THE LITTLE MONSTERS

Alan Bowne

BROADWAY PLAY PUBLISHING INC
New York
www.broadwayplaypublishing.com
info@broadwayplaypublishing.com

THE LITTLE MONSTERS
© Copyright 2018 Estate of Alan Bowne

Cover photo of the author in Montreal in 1972.

First edition: February 2018
I S B N: 978-0-88145-759-9

Book design: Marie Donovan
Page make-up: Adobe InDesign
Typeface: Palatino

CHARACTERS

MAURICE, *a bald myopic WASP in his late 50s*

KIP, *a slight plain scruffy male in his late teens; of Irish extraction*

3-YARD, *a coarse handsome well-built male in his late teens; of Italian extraction*

GOOEY, *a plump flashy Jewish female in her late teens—a hitter*

SETTING

Time: middle of summer, the present

A single set: a Lower East Side apartment. One dingy room stuffed to the gills with printed matter. Looks like a recycling center.

The room's skeleton consists of miscellaneous furniture, old and battered. A refrigerator and a stove; sink and counter— all clustered against one wall, with cabinets above flanking a window that looks out on an expanse of greyish brick. The sink is the tenement kind, deep and low, used for washing dishes as well as for taking baths. (The toilet's communal; it's on the landing.) Entry door from landing, against back wall; door, other wall, leads off to darkened bedroom.

Draping this skeleton is paper, paper everywhere and on everything. Great stacks of magazines and newspapers rise high as a man; the furniture groans under stacks of tabloid; the floor is a maze of boxed and bundled newsprint. The stacks, however, are neat, the bundles meticulously tied. Daily newspapers, dazzling glossies, weeklies, scandal rags, junk mail, flyers, professional brochures, pamphlets. Distinct mounds of clippings variously on floor and furniture. Stacks of 8 X 10 file boxes. A massive sort of order to all this: brochures lie in the vicinity of other brochures, and the magazines do not interbreed with the newspapers.

A path has been cut through from the entry door to stage center, and thence to kitchen area. The paper canyons form a rough semicircle around an open space downstage center, into which the actors may freely move.

A NOTE TO THE ACTORS

The unusual spelling and punctuation are intentional: they are the author's means of "scoring" the script.

MAURICE *speaks an East Coast intellectual's English that is breathless and "busy", one thought crowding upon another. Rattling enunciation.*

The kids speak a New York City blue-collar idiom that is a mixture of Queens, Brooklyn and the Lower East, the delivery of which is rapid and spitfire.

Delivery is indicated by the punctuation within speeches: internal periods do not indicate full stops, they indicate the staccato breathing specific to this idiom, the rhythmic, clipped hiatuses of New York speech. Similarly, an absence of internal punctuation indicates delivery in one breath.

ACT ONE

Scene 1: Afternoon

Scene 2: A few moments later

ACT TWO

Evening

ACT ONE

Scene 1

(Afternoon. Summer in New York City)

(The curtain rises on MAURICE, *thin bare shanks showing under a superannuated robe, seated center stage before a rickety T V tray covered with clippings. He is carefully scissoring articles from an old New York* Post. *Operatic music is blaring from a portable radio atop a pile of coupons on one of the burners of the stove: the trumpet solo from* Parsifal. *Occasionally, with his scissors, he conducts to the music.)*

(Shortly there is a knocking at the door.)

*(*MAURICE *listens, startled, head cocked. Another knocking. He stands, crosses carefully among the newsprint to the stove, lowers volume on radio.)*

MAURICE: *(Loudly)* Who! *(Softly)* In the world? *(Again loudly)* Is it?

VOICE: *(Offstage)* Lemme me in it's me.

*(*MAURICE *crosses to entrance door. Considers, stroking his chin reflectively)*

MAURICE: *(Loudly)* Let you in it's you. Meaning: Let you in *because* it's you? Or let you in. Period. It's you?

VOICE: *(Offstage. Exasperated:)* Maurice you fuck.

MAURICE: *(Same) Maurice you fuck?* Meaning: Maurice comma you expletive? Or meaning: Maurice comma you occasionally give way to your passions question mark?

VOICE: *(Offstage. Urgent:)* It's me you know it's Kip.

MAURICE: *(Same)* Who? I don't believe I know any— *(Crisply, enunciating the "p" sound)* Kip.

KIP: *(Offstage. Angrily:)* Lemme fuckin in!

MAURICE: *(Considering)* Fucking. In? Let you fuck in what? *(Beat)* Do you want to do that? In here? *(Beat)* Do you want to do that? To me?

KIP: *(Offstage, angrily rattling door:)* Maurice!

MAURICE: *(Dramatically)* An old fellow with a. *(Hand over chest)* Heart condition?

(Silence. Then:)

KIP: *(Offstage)* You lemme in or. See. I'm gonna stand here. See. Until you go out for eggs? Because you live on eggs. And then. When you go out for eggs? I'll be here. And—

(MAURICE yanks open door.)

(KIP pauses, looking at MAURICE.)

KIP: The fuck! Is this? Maurice.

(MAURICE abruptly kisses KIP lightly on his lips and closes door.)

MAURICE: *(Brightly)* Well. Hello, stranger.

(KIP moves through the paper ravines, his eyes darting about the room, then under the sink.)

MAURICE: *(Mock-salacious)* I said. Well. Stranger. Hello.

KIP: *(Looking under sink)* Stop it, you sound like. Like a farty old tart. Where's my gear?

MAURICE: *(Savouring words)* A farty. Old. Tart.

KIP: *(Straightening up)* So did you uh. Go and move any stuff around in this in here?

MAURICE: Of course not. Now. How are you? I trust you're in the pink?

KIP: *(Peering more closely under sink) Def'unly.* Only I had some gear under this. In a shoebox. You seen it?

MAURICE: Haven't seen *you* in ever so long. *(Punctuates by snipping scissors in air)* I expected. At the very least. A brief. Heartfelt. Hug. Nothing. Elaborate. You. Under. Stand.

KIP: *(Shrugging)* It's suckin hot, Maurice.

MAURICE: *(One final snip)* Ah.

KIP: *(Looking about for a chair)* Jesus. Can't I sit down even? *(Pointing to papers on a chair)* Can I move this shit? So we can talk?

MAURICE: *(Abruptly hard)* Don't touch that.

KIP: I wanna sit down.

MAURICE: *(Abruptly factual)* You want a glass of milk. Is what you want.

(MAURICE crosses to fridge, opens it, removes milk bottle.)

KIP: *(Exasperated)* I can't even! In this dizzy muck of shit! Sit down here!

MAURICE: *(Slams milk bottle on counter; restraining anger)* Dizzy. Muck of shit. *(Shrugs, pours milk into glass)* Everything here is in its appropriate place. *(Replaces bottle in fridge)* Everything here. Is organized. I've told you that repeatedly.

KIP: Then I must of got it wrong.

MAURICE: I've told you. And 3-Yard. And—

KIP: See I thought. You never moved nothin here.

MAURICE: And that girl. 3-Yard's girl. What's her name again? Fooey?

KIP: Gooey. With the jugs. You don't never move nothin here, right?

MAURICE: Even boy prostitutes have groupies these days, but I wish he wouldn't bring her here. She's vulgar.

KIP: Gooey's a hairdresser and I ast you a question.

MAURICE: A hairdresser. That explains it. You and 3-Yard are often crude but never. *(Smiles, holds out glass of milk)* Vulgar.

KIP: *Def* unly. But 3-Yard is dominator, so—

MAURICE: Indeed. *(Indicating glass)* Here. Knock it back.

KIP: *(Ignoring glass)* 3-Yard is comin here today, Maurice. So. So I. *(Bends again, looking under sink, then straightening up)* Can't find here. A thing here. Is the bo-de-o-do of today, Maurice.

(MAURICE, shaking his head, crosses to T V tray, clears a corner of it, places milk down, indicates his own chair.)

MAURICE: Here. I'll stand. You just come over here. Sit down. And drink it right up.

KIP: *(Watching him, then pointing at a chair)* Why can't I sit down here, Maurice?

MAURICE: Because that chair. *(Crisply, as before)* Kip. *(Normal)* Is women's rights.

(KIP looks nastily at chair.)

MAURICE: And your sneakered little feet. Are planted on a portion at least. Of civil rights. Black civil rights.

KIP: *(Looking at floor)* This here. This shit down here. Is some kinna—

(Overlapping)

MAURICE: Your very tattered, grungy little sneakers—

KIP: Some suckin buncha

MAURICE: Are planted smack in the middle of the struggle black people have waged—

KIP: *(Poking papers with toe)* Buncha bullshit about a buncha

MAURICE: For the last twenty-five years. As reported in the media—

KIP: Fuckin niggerheads—

MAURICE: The media large and small, major and obscure—

KIP: *(Indicating chair beside him)* And this is bitches and. *(Pointing)* What's that pile?

MAURICE: Selectively and chronologically organized. *(Beat)* That? Is gay rights.

KIP: Oh sure why not? *(Pointing around)* Bitches. Niggers. And queers.

MAURICE: *(Hard)* Stop using those words.

KIP: You better face up, Maurice. All this mess here in this is—

MAURICE: *(Exploding)* This is not! A mess!

(Silence)

(MAURICE wraps robe tighter about him; fidgets by making and unmaking fists; KIP looks in exasperation at ceiling.)

MAURICE: This. For your information. And for 3-Yard and Gooey's information. For the information of every lost illiterate brat abandoned by your parents and the educational system—

KIP: *(Pacing)* Don't get iced up here, Maurice.

MAURICE: Of this sad and woebegone. For the information of every. *(Gropes)* Every little hustler and merciless stinking pimple-assed achingly touchingly ill-mannered. *(Gropes again)* Who has ever camped out here or spit up here into my hand or. *(Clenching fists)*

This is not a mess! This is everything significant in your time that you will die and know nothing about. This is everything you would need to know in order *not!* To go on. And on. In one *ignorant!* Repetition! After! Another! *This! (Beat)* Is history.

KIP: *(Glum)* History.

MAURICE: This. Is an archive.

KIP: *(Trying to pronounce)* Ar. Kives. *(Shakes head)* Jesus. Looks like to me? A buncha old newspapers and I can't find my gear!

MAURICE: You will *find* here! Printed matter detailing significant contemporary facts which. In and of themselves! *(Loud whisper)* Do not reveal so much as a *single* connection. But! *(Beat)* This room. *(Crisply)* Kip. *(Resumes) Is* the connection. So *arranged.* As to reveal the significant data. Grouped by subject and cross-referenced in my file boxes. *(Pointing about room; emphatic)* Women's rights. Black people's rights. Passive resistance. Freedom of the press. The military. Nuclear disarmament. *(Slight pause)* Odd sorts of. Sex murders. *(Emphatic again)* The drug traffic. The presidency. The Right. The Left. The economy. And. So. On! *(He has quieted somewhat, but still trembles.)* So when you. Or 3-Yard. Or any other cheap.

KIP: *(Bored, tapping his foot, looking about)* Yeah?

MAURICE: Boy. Or.

KIP: Hooker. You mean hooker. Say hooker.

MAURICE: *(Indicating room, then bedroom)* So when you come in here, you will leave things exactly as they are. You may sleep on my bed or on the bedroom floor, you may pass out on my bed or grunt and sweat with your. Girlfriends!

KIP: While you watch.

MAURICE: But in here you will not! Move a single. Piece. Of *history*. *(Calmly)* Now drink your milk.

KIP: *(Conciliating)* Hey. Maurice.

MAURICE: Please. Drink your milk.

KIP: I asked you before. You seen a box around here?

MAURICE: No. There's a young actor on television. Who thinks drinking milk, is here to stay.

KIP: Like I said. A shoebox. Tied up. Got some of my gear in it.

MAURICE: He's a remarkably cute boy. And he has made it clear that milk. Is here, for the duration.

KIP: You seen this? This box of mine?

MAURICE: No, I have not. So sit over here and drink up.

KIP: I stuck it under the sink only now it ain't there. I just stuck it back there can I take a look?

MAURICE: *(Shrugging)* He's much cuter than you. And he drinks *lots* of milk.

KIP: Uh-huh. That actor? *(Pointing under sink)* Can I look? *(He bends, peers under sink.)* That actor?

MAURICE: Yes?

KIP: Should have a can of Budweiser. *(Rising up)* Shoved up his tubes *(No pause)* so where's my box?

MAURICE: Your box.

KIP: What I said.

MAURICE: This alleged box. Was left here?

KIP: Yeah. Last time I was over.

MAURICE: That would be. Let me see.

KIP: Last week.

MAURICE: Yes, last week. An entire week. Hard to remember. *(Coyly)* Well. I've had so many boys up here. Since last week.

KIP: You what?

MAURICE: A constant stream. I've been very passionate.

KIP: You had other guys up here? You mean like strange guys?

MAURICE: *(Considering)* Strange?

KIP: Like P Rs and shit?

MAURICE: I am not, like you, a bigot. I am generous with my.

KIP: *Up here?*

MAURICE: *(Defensive)* I. Yes.

KIP: When me. And 3-Yard. And even that Gooey his girlfriend. Come here. As your *guest?*

MAURICE: Yes, whenever you needed a place to flop.

KIP: And not know. That we could get picked off. Any time. By some *uglyass?*

MAURICE: Or when you needed money.

KIP: Who has made a map! Of this apartment here? While.

MAURICE: Or a decent meal.

KIP: While he was stickin his dongalong in your lippy chops. Is that the feature?

MAURICE: Kip, I am hardly the type to.

KIP: Bitch, we was your *guest!*

MAURICE: To pick up some godzilla. Some. And I am also.

KIP: I thought you was *specialty.*

MAURICE: Known. In this. Neighborhood!

KIP: *(Enraged)* You slutty faggot you brung. To this apartment? Where I was keepin my gear? *Some fuckin some blackass jujube P R fuckhead? (He plunges to knees, rummages under sink.)*

*(*MAURICE *tosses head, snips air with scissors, sits in chair, determinedly clips articles with scissors.)*

MAURICE: I am very sorry to hear you. Use those. Words.

*(*KIP *sits back on haunches, desperately looks about.)*

MAURICE: After all, Kip, where? I ask you, where? Would you be without us— "faggots"?

KIP: *(Over shoulder)* I ditn't say this. About queens. You! Was my old queen. *(Stands, paces along paths)* You! Was my mark. I would share you with 3-Yard but on the bottom of it *you!* Was my steady mark who *said!* She was so weird about disease.

MAURICE: *(Wielding scissors)* It was only. One boy. I lied. It wasn't exactly a stream. I can't afford a stream. It was more like a dribble.

KIP: *(Halting)* One hooker?

MAURICE: *(Same)* You know I have a heart condition.

KIP: Oh yeah right.

MAURICE: And you weren't around and.

KIP: A big muddy number like around Avenue D?

MAURICE: *(Slightly bridling)* No. I told you. A young boy. Black, yes. In a New York Mets baseball cap. I met him in Tomkins Square. It was a hot day and I.

KIP: A faggy sorta nigger?

MAURICE: I took a walk. I went out to shop and decided I would sit under the trees. The wretched. And blasted. Trees. In Tomkins Square. And this boy.

KIP: Now! If it was a faggy twinkie kinna black, that's okay. I could deal with this I work with this.

MAURICE: Well, yes. He was very sweet. In his way.

KIP: Not one of these meatpackers offa Avenue D. This was a twinkie. You could point him out to me.

MAURICE: I don't know. I'm afraid he was just another straight kid who plays. Ball. Shirtless. In Tomkins Square. I doubt he would take anything. He was broke. Of course.

KIP: *(Throwing up hands)* A amateur! You brung this hungry amateur to your apartment?

MAURICE: Drink your milk.

KIP: Who steals *my* gear. When I was this *guest!* In your apartment.

MAURICE: I'm sure he took nothing.

KIP: You're sure?

MAURICE: He was a trifle rough. Around the edges? But mainly what he wanted. Was to earn his twenty bucks and get out of here.

KIP: *Twenny bucks?* For a amateur? Lady, you are somethin! I thought. *(Helpless gesture)* What I thought was I could trust you.

MAURICE: Then don't leave me alone.

KIP: You would do this to me. Your own husband.

MAURICE: A husband! *(Crisply)* Kip! *(Normal)* Doesn't just. Come and go.

KIP: So I was busy!

MAURICE: I would appreciate a little consideration.

KIP: This ain't my apartment? You said. Use it.

MAURICE: As long! As you disturb nothing in here.

KIP: Jesus, Maurice. *(Squats, hugs knees)* How many old ladies. Onna Lower East. With the pisser down the hall usually some old spic is in there? Has got herself a young white guy onna regular thing he's no fag and don't charge her for every poke?

(MAURICE does not respond.)

KIP: I mean, I been pretty good to you, Maurice. I let you talk at me all this *(Indicates room with chin)* history and this and shove eggs in my face and. And. *(Points at sink)* Member that time I took a bath in this sink and you made cookies for me? *(No response)* And I set you up with 3-Yard who is first of all a dominator and second he's a looker so says you. So why you go and fuck it face down like I was some kinna. Some kinna. Some kinna my gear is just a sack of garbage?

MAURICE: *Never leave me alone! (Beat)* For a whole week again. *(He resumes scissoring.)*

(KIP grabs newspaper from MAURICE's hands, crumples it.)

KIP: Fuckin you are up to your *tits*! In this shitty. Paper!

MAURICE: Give that back!

(KIP casts newspaper to floor.)

KIP: And you are lucky as suckall to have me, Maurice!

(MAURICE falls to knees, grabs paper.)

MAURICE: *(Trying to put newspaper back together)* I *hate* this. When.

KIP: Livin off your disability and what your mother had stashed.

MAURICE: *(Rustling paper)* I hate it when things get—

KIP: No job just sit here *(Scissor gestures with fingers)* snippy snippy snippy?

MAURICE: *(Sitting again; rustling paper)* Get so goddamned—

KIP: Mosta my johns usually got real good jobs, Maurice!

MAURICE: *(Casting paper from him in despair)* Disorganized!

(Pause)

(Breathing hard, MAURICE *begins clenching and unclenching fists.* KIP *watches him.)*

MAURICE: I have arranged here. Each clipping and news item. One upon the other in chronological. Grouped by subject. *(Gropes; gives up)* Drink your milk. Go into the bedroom. Watch T V. And drink your.

KIP: I ain't movin.

MAURICE: Milk. And leave me.

KIP: Til I get my gear.

MAURICE: Alone. I haven't got your.

KIP: I know you ain't got it. Some amateur has got it he plays ball? With the naked nipples? On Tomkins Square. *(Tired singsong)* So what we gotta do.

MAURICE: I never left him for a minute. He couldn't have stolen a.

KIP: *(Same)* Is go down to the Square. And hang out inna heat. Til this ape shows up. With the New York Mets.

MAURICE: I was with him! Every! Minute!

KIP: *(Same)* And the hot pink pecs.

MAURICE: That he was here. Every instant! *(Crisply)* Kip.

KIP: *(Intently)* You know this. For a fact? You never turned your back on him?

MAURICE: Why in the world? He was beautiful to look at.

KIP: *(Gesturing towards landing)* You didn't go down the hall to the can?

MAURICE: *(Calmly snipping away)* Much more beautiful than you will ever be.

KIP: So Maurice? Where's my gear?

MAURICE: Unlike your spotty. Splotchy. Red and yoghurt skin. His was. I think the phrase is cafe au lait. Very smooth. Flawless, in fact.

KIP: I put it to you a question.

MAURICE: He had no pimples. No hairs growing *out* of pimples.

KIP: So Maurice?

MAURICE: Indeed very little body hair at all. Just this. Above his. Tight little clusters of pubic hair.

KIP: See. You don't get it.

MAURICE: Like brush on a.

KIP: What I'm talkin here.

MAURICE: On a savannah. In Nairobi.

(Pause)

KIP: He got *what*?

MAURICE: On an African. Savannah.

KIP: Some kinna *what*?

MAURICE: Clean and dry and smelling like. Chapperal. On a plain. In Africa.

(Pause)

KIP: *(Wide-eyed contempt)* You see any lions in there? Any bears?

MAURICE: How anyone! With skin like yours. The color of hepatitis under a *sunlamp*! Could look at a black kid.

KIP: *(Incredulous)* His *dick* hair? You're talkin his *dick* hair?

MAURICE: A smooth and finished. Product of nature. And say.

KIP: Maurice, I gotta put it to you.

MAURICE: *(Scissoring faster now)* That *he's* inferior. Is so. So utterly and patently ridiculous!

KIP: You, Maurice. Are onna Canarsie Line. You took a subway. To Disney World.

MAURICE: You with your ill-proportioned leached-out matted sweaty cold pudding soft *(Stops snipping; raises both hands and scissors over head)* DRINK YOUR MILK!

(KIP crosses to MAURICE, picks up glass, crosses to sink.)

KIP: *(Leaning against sink; calmly pouring milk into sink behind him)* See, Maurice, we got a problem.

MAURICE: *(Staring)* Don't you ever eat or drink *anything* that's good for you?

KIP: *(Gestures with empty glass)* And the problem is this.

MAURICE: *(Snipping again)* When you consider the nutritional *deficiencies.*

KIP: 3-Yard is comin here. And when he finds out. *(He gestures warningly with glass; then looks at it.)*

MAURICE: And yet! That same boy, that black kid who came to visit?, He probably eats the same junk that you eat.

KIP: *(Looking at glass; then looking around)* Hey. What do I do with this?

MAURICE: Only *look* at the difference!

KIP: You can't sit nothin down here. Paper. Paper. Everywhere you got piles of it.

MAURICE: Meaning: There is obviously a genetic! Superiority! Among blacks.

KIP: Hey, Maurice.

MAURICE: Unblemished. Firm. Smooth. Beautifully proportioned. Despite! MacDonald's. Any race! That can survive MacDonald's. And *still* be beautiful—!

KIP: Maurice you asshole! I'm askin you *where! Do I hang this fuckin glass? (Pause)*

MAURICE: You know very well. The cabinet on the left is for dirty dishes, the one on the right is for clean.

KIP: *(Opening cabinet)* What's this? *(He withdraws a handful of paper strips.)*

MAURICE: Those are. I think. Comic strips.

KIP: *(Looking at them) Dagwood? Doonesbury? Poodie the Poodle?*

MAURICE: *(Calmly scissoring)* They relate. To the washing of dishes. When I'm depressed about doing the dishes, I read them. They make me feel better.

(KIP stares at MAURICE, then thrusts comics and glass into cabinet and slams shut the cabinet door.)

KIP: Maurice. *(He crosses to MAURICE, bends forward, grips T V tray; into MAURICE's face:)* I'm tellin you. We gotta find my gear. 3-Yard's comin here and—

MAURICE: *(Shrugs)* So I'll scramble some eggs.

KIP: *(Withdrawing)* Now can I move some of this shit and look for my gear? Before he comes here?

MAURICE: No, you may not.

(KIP picks up a bundle, moves it downstage.)

MAURICE: *(Alarmed; rising)* What are you doing?

KIP: *(Returning for another bundle)* I'm just gonna put it over here for right now. Then I'll move it back.

MAURICE: You will do nothing of the sort!

(MAURICE *crosses to displaced bundle, picks it up. During following,* KIP *and* MAURICE *cross and re-cross carrying the same bundles.*)

KIP: I'm gonna look around over on this side and then—

MAURICE: Stop it! You are mixing up the *Newsweeks*! With the *Village Voices*!

KIP: 3-Yard's gonna be mad, Maurice, he finds out you lost my gear.

MAURICE: That! has been chronologically *arranged*.

KIP: Dominator do not like it! When one of his men! Gets his *gear* taken off!

MAURICE: He won't care in the least! Where are you going with that?

KIP: See, if I ain't safe here, then he ain't safe here. Get me? 3-Yard's a hater, Maurice!

(MAURICE *grabs bundle in* KIP's *arms, holds on to it; into* KIP's *face*)

MAURICE: 3-Yard! is a lot of hot air—!

KIP: Let it go, Maurice!

MAURICE: Bad breath—!

KIP: Suckin suck off, Maurice!

MAURICE: Dirty behind—!

KIP: You got off on it!

MAURICE: No education—! *(Beat)* I *beg* your pardon?

KIP: That time I let him session your ass? Member, Maurice?

MAURICE: That! Was just. *(Tossing head; quickly)* A *frisson*.

KIP: Don't talk Spanish at me, Maurice, and get your claws off a here!

(MAURICE *yanks bundle away.*)

MAURICE: *(Looking about)* Now where did you get this?

KIP: *(Grabs bundle again)* Give it here, Maurice!

MAURICE: *(Struggling)* No education! No direction! Smelly pits! A set of blunted instincts—!

KIP: *(Struggling)* He's a killer and a hater, Maurice, and he's gonna rattle your ovaries and it *ain't!* gonna be like a session.

MAURICE: *(Same)* Three pair of khaki pants! A leather vest! And he won't! care! about your silly shoebox. He doesn't even *like* you!

(Beat. KIP *stares, clutching bundle.)*

KIP: What do you mean he don't?

MAURICE: He treats you like dirt. He doesn't care about you. *Nobody* cares about you! *(Yanks away bundle)* Nobody, Kip. But me.

*(*KIP *and* MAURICE *stare.)*

*(*KIP *looks away, then back at* MAURICE.*)*

KIP: That is a fuckin. That is a fuckin. *(Finger in* MAURICE's *face)* He's dominator, that's all. Every organization gotta have a dominator!

*(*MAURICE *replaces bundle, crosses downstage for another,* KIP *watching him.)*

MAURICE: A long dumb noisy Italian.

KIP: *(Placating)* Look, Maurice.

MAURICE: With a daffy little Jewish girlfriend.

KIP: Maurice?

MAURICE: A great slurpy slavering dong that thuds when he walks.

KIP: Will you lissen at me, Maurice?

(MAURICE *replaces bundle, goes for another.*)

MAURICE: *(Indicating* KIP*)* Who lords it over a confused frightened Irish punk! *(Returns with bundle)* And has a life expectancy of about nineteen! *I* think. He's funny.

KIP: *(Grabbing bundle)* Laugh yourself to death, Maurice!

MAURICE: *(Struggling)* He *has* no power! If only you'd *learn* from me!

KIP: *(Struggling)* Nothin to learn, Maurice!

MAURICE: *(Same)* And from the collective experience of others! Of *which*—give it here! —this! *(Yanks away bundle, replaces it)* Is an example.

KIP: Oh. Okay. *(He grabs another bundle, carries it away.)*

MAURICE: Not *that*! It's been indexed!

(KIP *and* MAURICE *struggle with bundle.*)

KIP: It's all poop, Maurice!

MAURICE: *Shhhhh!*

(MAURICE *freezes; so does* KIP.)

MAURICE: Listen to that!

KIP: What?

MAURICE: *(Loud whisper)* To the music, Kip.

KIP: *(Also in whisper)* Fuckin what music, Maurice?

MAURICE: *(Same)* The clue, Kip. Is in the music.

KIP: *(Sharp; suspicious)* The *clue*?

MAURICE: *(Loud whisper)* To history. *(He tiptoes with bundle back to where it was, replaces it, straightens stack.)* *(Same)* There's power here. Symphonic. Omniscient.

KIP: English! Talk English!

MAURICE: *Shhhhh!* If only you'd listen to the music.
You could rise above the street, be worth a thousand
3-Yards.

KIP: I gotta find. A clue? In this garbage.

MAURICE: It's not. *Garbage!* There's an order here—
unseen by most people, because it's like music. Under
all this discord is a sublime and powerful composition.
Moving through time. It's all harmony and intellect,
knowledge and understanding. Occasionally people
listen. And when they do, they achieve the little.
Heroisms. That I've documented here. But every now
and then, Kip, a figure arises who is attuned to the
music of greatness, who gathers that symphonic power
into himself, and explodes into history. There's a little
bit of the hero in all of us, Kip. Even in you. *(Sweeps
room with hand)* That's what all of this means. *(Exalted)*
Galileo and Ghandi. Alexander, Caesar and Napoleon.
John. Fitzgerald. *Kennedy! (Points down at bundles)* This
entire stack is devoted to that man.

KIP: Maurice?

MAURICE: Kip?

KIP: Where— *(Exploding) Do you live???*

*(KIP grabs another bundle, starts carrying it away;
MAURICE also grabs it.)*

MAURICE: If only you'd let me teach you! Empower
you!

KIP: You just yak away here! Like some anchorhead!
Onna six o'clock news!

MAURICE: I am *far* better informed, *far* better organized,
than the six o'clock news!

KIP: Springin for niggers rattle about the fairies' rights!
But *my* gear? *My* rights?

MAURICE: You're just jealous jealous jealous! Of that black kid.

*(*KIP *pauses in the struggle. Incredulous:)*

KIP: You think. You think that that's. That that's.

MAURICE: *(Mimicking)* Dat-dat. Dat-dat.

KIP: That that's. Shut up!

*(*KIP *and* MAURICE *resume struggle over bundle.)*

MAURICE: Now that black kid. *He* was hero material. Why, he hardly—give it here! —uttered a stupidity. He was alert. Poised. Attuned. Listening to the music—

KIP: *(Into* MAURICE's *face) He was turnin a trick! (He yanks bundle from* MAURICE; *calmer:)* Look, Maurice.

MAURICE: Put that back, Kip.

KIP: I'm doin this for your own good, Maurice.

MAURICE: Put it. Back.

KIP: Cause see. You my old girlfriend, right? You my steady or what? I mean. See. I don't want nothin bad to happen all over your ass. See. And. So. *(Gropes; looks away)* Nothin should come in here. And *hurt* you, Maurice.

(Beat. MAURICE *looks fondly at* KIP, *pecks the boy on the lips)*

MAURICE: Thank you, Kip. See? There's a lot of good in you. *(Then he violently yanks away bundle.)* But I *won't* have this room disorganized!

*(*KIP *throws up his hands and turns away, as* MAURICE *replaces bundle.)*

(Suddenly there is a loud, tumultuous pounding at the door.)

KIP: *(Freezing; startled)* It's 3-Yard!

MAURICE: *(Unconcerned, surveying stack)* There.

(Satisfied, MAURICE *returns to T V tray and sits. Pounding resumes.)*

MAURICE: *(Snipping away)* I'm waiting, Kip. For my hero.

(KIP *watches* MAURICE, *as pounding resumes, loud and seismic.)*

(Blackout)

Scene 2

(The same, a moment or two later. As curtain rises:)

(MAURICE *is seated at T V tray, snipping away as before.* KIP *is standing by sink, warily watching* 3-YARD.)

(3-YARD *is standing downstage center, facing audience. His palm is open before him and onto it he traces imaginary words with his finger.)*

3-YARD: *(Referring to palm)* It says here? People with brats are dickheads. Dickheads with kids? Talk like morons *(No pause; turns from audience, swaggers towards* KIP*)* today I'm sittin this sidewalk coffee place on Saint Marks I'm mindin my face and havin a doppio. Next table's a coupla young marrieds? So white you could go blind and they shit money.

KIP: 3-Yard?

(3-YARD *saunters back to face audience, knocking over a small bundle of newspapers as he does so.* MAURICE *reacts to this by holding scissors aloft, in a silent rage.)*

3-YARD: *(To audience again)* Where. Do they come from? Why. Are they here? And they got their baby girl at the table. This five-year-old acts like a drug dealer? They give *birth* to this! This with the teensy weeny fingernails tappin onna tabletop and givin orders like a fuckin prima diva? And they suck *up* to it! It hisses *back* at them! Like, who *are* these moronics? They're sittin there in my ear all about cannoli *(No pause; cloying)* you wanna cannoli? Dorothy? You want some gelati? *(Normal)* They go on with this lime moka gelati for about two hours this five-year-old peepee face could lick some annisette offa my *boot!*

(MAURICE has risen from chair, replaced bundle.)

MAURICE: *(Sitting again and resuming; muttering)* Knuckle-walking ape.

3-YARD: *(Same)* This neighborhood is runnin down here. Usta be you seen only the fat old Roosian bimbos the stumblebums and a coupla lowlife punkasses. Now? You got people walkin around from Long Island? Wearin a coupla hunnert dollars of the suckiest nurdie fash and *socks!* You gotta come way over here at Alphabet to find one real humanoid. Saint Marks? Got Zen Buddhist cafes it got people on *dates!* It got a lotta rock 'n rollers from N-Y-fuckin-U there is nothin! More stupid than a rock 'n roll musician we are talkin brain pans of maybe two square centimeters here.

KIP: I said, 3-Yard?

3-YARD: *(Same)* Only thing more dumb than a base guitarist? Is a photographer! These! are holeheads. Fuckin rock 'n roll photographers and pussy fags wall to roof and fuck me on Second Avenue. In a coupla years? You prob'ly can stuff your face at a wine and cookie bar on *Delancey Street!* And *then* you can stick balloons on Tomkins Square and sailit to New Jersey cause this! *(Holding up palm, tracing words)* Is the Lower East Side today.

(Beat)

KIP: *(Swallowing hard)* Maurice don't got it, 3-Yard!

(Pause)

(3-YARD, *still holding up palm, looks at audience, then over shoulder at* KIP.)

(MAURICE *continues snipping away; a studied indifference.*)

KIP: It ain't here now. *(Desperately; indicating* MAURICE*)* She lost it.

(Pause, as 3-YARD *looks straight at audience, drops hand, flexes shoulders. Slowly holds up palm again, and traces words onto it with his finger)*

3-YARD: Okay. It says here. The guy who messes onna delivery? Is very sucked. *(Turns from audience; approaches* KIP*)* Here. You wanna read it? It says. What it says is. Lootenants like you. Drop things onna floor? Look. It says right here. *(Sticks palm in* KIP*'s face)*

KIP: *(Looking away)* Hey.

3-YARD: *(Same)* Look. It's right here in black and white.

KIP: *(Same)* Dominator hey!

3-YARD: It *says*—!

(3-YARD *strikes* KIP *full in the face;* KIP *crashes against refrigerator.*)

MAURICE: Stop it! *(He rises and crosses to* KIP*; squats beside him.)*

(3-YARD *composes himself by leaning on sink. He speaks out the window:)*

3-YARD: Okay. Now. *Who!* Is dominator?

*(*KIP *is struggling to regain his feet;* MAURICE *examines the boy's lip.)*

KIP: You are.

3-YARD: Do I hear some Irish nigger tellin me. I am dominator?

KIP: So?

*(*KIP *is on his feet,* MAURICE *clucking over him.)*

3-YARD: Some Irish *tootsun'* usta live in Stuy Town? His mother was keypunch she won't even go probation on him?

KIP: *(Placating; waving* MAURICE *away)* Hey. 3-Yard. Dip it. Okay?

3-YARD: *Do I hear this? (Turns; points at* MAURICE*)* Sayin. Me and this old nautch queen over here. Is standin around with our panties fulla poop. Sayin this. To dominator?

MAURICE: *(To* 3-YARD*)* You. Are ridiculous.

*(*MAURICE *returns to T V tray and sits, resuming;* 3-YARD *trains his finger on* KIP*.)*

KIP: It's gotta be here. Only. *(Gestures helplessly at room)* I don't know where.

3-YARD: You don't. Know. Where. *(Nods, still pointing)* That's good. Then I heard it right? All that I said?

KIP: It's gotta *be* here!

MAURICE: *(To* 3-YARD*; suppressed rage; punctuated by snipping)* You come in here! You pound on my door and you come in here. Like a clumsy. Matted. Wildebeest! You bellow and roar and hit people and. Stand here. Nodding your empty head. As if! You had a thought. Some lurching. Glutinous. Half-born thought. That you are trying! To shit out! Through your great! thick! constipated! ears!

3-YARD: *(As if he hasn't heard)* You got a Gimbels' charge card?

MAURICE: *(Exasperated; setting down scissors)* All right, Kip.

3-YARD: *(To* MAURICE*)* I ast you a question.

MAURICE: What. *(Crisply)* Kip. *(Normal)* Was in the shoebox?

3-YARD: A Gimbels or a Macy's? A Super Saver Account?

KIP: Close your face, Maurice.

MAURICE: *(To* KIP*)* What did you hide in here?

3-YARD: For what you lost in here you better have. About six bank accounts insured innerest onna three percent government loan with IRA and kuggerants and shit. That! *(Beat; finger in* MAURICE*'s face)* Is what you better have, Maurice.

MAURICE: *(Brushing away* 3-YARD*'s finger)* I'll scramble some eggs. *(To* KIP*)* While you. Cook up an answer.

*(*MAURICE *crosses to kitchenette and proceeds to crack eggs into a bowl.* 3-YARD *shifts his finger ominously in the direction of* KIP*.)*

3-YARD: She says. This old pussy you had her snatched she would do for you? She just said. *(Holds out palm)* It's right here. I took it down. *(Reads palm)* I. Am no kinna. Fag hole. For this Irish. Nigger. *(Extends palm to* KIP*)* See?

KIP: She'll *do* for me!

3-YARD: *(To* KIP*)* Control here. Is what I don't hear here. *(Picks up a* New York *magazine from a stack)* In all this? With the *New York* magazines how you can make cheese pie with Liz Taylor?

*(*MAURICE *spins round and gasps as* 3-YARD *drops the* New York *and picks up a* Village Voice*.)*

3-YARD: Or this it goes boo-hoo over Ethiopials? *(Casts* Village Voice *to floor)*

MAURICE: How *dare* you!

*(*MAURICE *rushes to replace publications as:)*

3-YARD: *(Jabbing finger about room)* In this with the *Newsday* and the *Timeweek* and the *Times Up* and the

News News and the *Daily News* and the *New York* and
the *York News* in alla this! Somewhere. Is a box. Of
which! No control. Is a taxation. On my. *(Gropes)* My.
Own. Conceptual. Of what it is. That you do. When.

MAURICE: *(Into 3-YARD's face) I am making scrambled
eggs!*

(Beat. MAURICE *returns to kitchenette and his eggs as*
3-YARD *looks ominously at* KIP.*)*

3-YARD: I don't hear. Control here.

KIP: *(Nervously)* What it was. She had this nigger up in
this.

3-YARD: Your fag lady. Popped some loose trade. In
your territory?

KIP: Is what it was. Yeah.

MAURICE: *(Fiercely stirring eggs)* Touch nothing in here.
Ever. *Again! (Pauses)* I'm out of Worcestershire.

3-YARD: *(Jabbing finger at* MAURICE*) You? (Approaches*
MAURICE*)* Would bring in here. Into the territory of
Caucasoids? Some darkface, some—

KIP: *(Interposing himself)* Will you leave her to me,
3-Yard?

3-YARD: *(Regarding* KIP*)* Who's pussy here? *(Indicating*
MAURICE*)* Is she pussy? Or is this one over at this? Is
this? Here? *(Jabbing finger into* KIP's *chest)* The stink of a
uterine device? Between the legs. Of a lootenant in the
service of dominator? *(He abruptly turns from* KIP, *calmly
sits at T V tray.)* We got a problem here. *(He casually
sweeps clippings from tray onto floor.)*

MAURICE: *(Dropping everything; shocked; to* 3-YARD*)*
You filthy! Ignorant— *(He makes, unmakes fists. Then
he surges forward, grips T V tray, shouting into* 3-YARD's
impassive face.) Get out! Out! Out!

*(*KIP *drags* MAURICE *away from tray.)*

(MAURICE *slaps* KIP'*s face, hard; to him:*)

MAURICE: You *are* a pussy! (*He turns, breathing hard, tears welling; he grips sink, then makes with the fists. Under his breath:*) God forgive me.

(KIP *stands where slapped, momentarily stunned.*)

3-YARD: So uh. (*Silence*) Like I figured. (*Silence*) Pussyslapped. (*Looks casually about room, ducking his head, peering, etc.*) Slapped. By. A female. Faggot. Queen. Pansytitted. Queer woman. With. Preparation H. In her chingasa. Where. Is. The shoebox?

(*Continues peering;* KIP *is breathing harder and harder.*)

3-YARD: That my fag lootenant. Shoved in here. When I thought. He was a real man. Now. Where? Is?

(KIP *suddenly grabs* MAURICE *from behind, forces him to his knees, thrusts his crotch in the older man's face.* KIP *then looks at* 3-YARD, *defiantly.*)

KIP: (*To* MAURICE, *but looking at* 3-YARD) Who bottom for me?

(MAURICE *struggles, face pressed to crotch of* KIP'*s jeans.*)

KIP: Huh? Who? Who?

(KIP *thrusts* MAURICE *to floor. Brutally kicks him in stomach*)

(MAURICE *screams in pain.*)

(3-YARD *stands, kicks away T V tray, pulls* MAURICE, *gasping with pain, into chair; into his face:*)

3-YARD: Maybe you need some discipline only you need it from a real man, hey? Is that it? Then you gonna tell us?

(KIP *is standing rigid; breathing hard.*)

MAURICE: (*To* 3-YARD; *gasping*) I. Don't know. You. Get out.

3-YARD: A real man is needed here. See, Maurice, I sorta thought. You *had* a man. I ditn't know you two was lesbos. I ditn't.

(KIP *suddenly breaks his rigid pose by wild gesticulation.*)

KIP: *Would you fuck off with this this this lezzie shit?*

MAURICE: I. Have. *A heart condition!*

3-YARD: *(To* KIP*)* She what?

KIP: She got this. Condition. In her fuckin heart.

3-YARD: I never notice. Maurice, I banged you around once a little. You ditn't say nothin about it.

MAURICE: That was. Different. That was. Controlled. I told you what I wanted. And I watched you do it. As if. *(Dreamily)* From a long. Way. Away.

(3-YARD *looks from* MAURICE *to* KIP*, wide-eyed. Indicating* MAURICE:*)*

3-YARD: *Twilight Zone.* The Movie.

MAURICE: But this! Is a violation. Of my being. You have destroyed. *(Looks mournfully at scattered clippings)* Months of careful. Referenced. organization.

3-YARD: Hey. Don't worry. We *gonna* get organized.

(3-YARD *strides to a bound stack of newspapers. Whips out switchblade, releases it, and slices through rope, sending papers spilling in all directions)*

(MAURICE *looks on in horror. Suddenly he leaps to his feet and throws himself on* 3-YARD*, pounding the boy's back with his fists, of course ineffectually.)*

3-YARD: *(Over his shoulder)* What *is* this shit?

(KIP *grasps* MAURICE *by tendons on back of neck and wrenches him painfully to the floor.)*

(MAURICE *cries out, is immobilized.)*

KIP: *(To* MAURICE; *through his teeth)* I warned you, Maurice.

3-YARD: *(To* KIP*)* Put her inna chair.

*(*KIP *drags* MAURICE *to chair and plumps him, groaning, into it.)*

*(*3-YARD *has the sliced rope in his hand. He ties* MAURICE *to the chair.)*

3-YARD: *(Into* MAURICE'S *face)* Now. You gonna get screamy?

MAURICE: I will. Take.

3-YARD: Take?

MAURICE: The roof.

3-YARD: The what?

MAURICE: *(Yelling)* THE ROOF OFF!

*(*KIP *intrudes, clasping hand over* MAURICE's *mouth.)*

KIP: Shut up, Maurice! *(Into* MAURICE's *face; loud whisper)* Did I warn you? Did I?

3-YARD: *(Pushing* KIP *aside; to* MAURICE*)* So. I gotta stuff a sock in your mouth hole?

MAURICE: *(Panicked)* No! *(Gasps)* I. Can't. Breathe very well. Through my nose. Don't. Please. Do that.

KIP: *(Nodding at* 3-YARD*)* Adenoids.

MAURICE: It's like dying. Like all one's apertures. All one's doors to the world. Are slammed—

3-YARD: *(Impatient)* Okay right.

MAURICE: —shut.

3-YARD: Okay so screamy is out, right?

MAURICE: Please don't. Do that.

(Beat)

KIP: So. *(Nods at* 3-YARD*)* She's no trouble, 3-Yard. See what I mean?

(Pause, as 3-YARD *glares at* KIP; *then points his rigid finger at him.)*

3-YARD: You!

KIP: Dominator. Listen.

3-YARD: Are on probabation!

(Pause)

KIP: *(Glumly)* Okay.

3-YARD: Okay what?

KIP: Okay *Sir.*

3-YARD: Now. *(He flexes shoulders.)* You are my second in command I gotta discipline this lady. I don't want words or back spit or maybe it's in Prospect Park. You feature?

KIP: I feature.

3-YARD: So. We get started. *(To* MAURICE; *sincere)* How you feelin?

MAURICE: *(Aghast)* Feeling?

3-YARD: Your adenoids. Your cardiacs. It's all in place? You wanna glass of milk?

MAURICE: *(Trying to be calm)* I want you. 3-Yard. To untie me. And go. You can come back. As in the past. And go into the bedroom. With Gooey. And fine. Just. Watch T V.

3-YARD: See but what it is. Is.

MAURICE: Whenever you need a place to sleep. Or. But right now.

3-YARD: *(Sincere)* Is this. I want you to be comfortable.

MAURICE: *(Dully)* Comfortable.

3-YARD: See because what we gotta do. Is find this thing here. *(Indicating room)* In this. This.

KIP: It's a ar. I mean. A kinna you know. A history place.

3-YARD: *(To MAURICE)* In this history place. And I want you should think about it and be comfortable.

(3-YARD crosses to a stack of file boxes. Empties three file drawers onto floor in rapid succession. Then he postures at MAURICE.)

MAURICE: *(Staring)* You! DAGO! *(Despairingly shaking his head, blinking away tears)* Look. What. You made me say.

3-YARD: Okay, Maurice. I been comin here a few times. Hey? When we was in the neighborhood. Me and Gooey. And I would come in here and go right through this. *(Groping; indicating room. Snaps fingers at KIP for assistance)* This.

KIP: History. Thing.

3-YARD: Yeah. I would come in here. And go inna bedroom and not think about it. I mean, it seemed a weirdness to me but who gives a dime I'll watch T V. Hey? Some old auntie with her clippers and her paper poopie it's the Lower East you make allowances. But!

MAURICE: I gave you money, 3-Yard. And eggs. And a place.

3-YARD: *(Sincerely)* Thanks for the scrambled eggs. *(Pause)* It was nice of you. But now. See? It's a new thing.

MAURICE: No.

3-YARD: It is. A new. Whole. Tutti-frutti.

MAURICE: Speak! English!

(Pause, as 3-YARD leans into MAURICE's face)

3-YARD: Thirt. Teen. Grams. Of dirt.

MAURICE: *(Uncertain)* Dirt.

(3-YARD nods.)

MAURICE: Meaning. Some kind of drug?

3-YARD: Some kinna. Yeah. Chemical. White. Powder.

MAURICE: You hid drugs in here. In a shoebox. Not? Marijuana.

3-YARD: No. I said to you. I said. Dirt. *(To KIP)* Ditn't I?

KIP: Sure. You said. *(Nods)* Yeah.

3-YARD: *(Extending palm to MAURICE)* I wrote it down.

MAURICE: How did you. *(Loud whisper)* You! *(Normal)* Get that much, I mean. That must be a lot of.

KIP: The dominator? He turns.

3-YARD: *(Proudly)* I set it up and lemme tell you. It went like silk. Only. It was unavoidable. I have injured some very important parties.

KIP: *(Nodding at MAURICE)* Syndicate. Very high up.

MAURICE: You stole. All those drugs. You. *(Shaken)* Must be in danger.

3-YARD: Not *today*! Not when we find that shoebox. See. *(Moves about)* Gooey is comin here. Later. With a Hertz-a-car. Okay? And tonight we will make our delivery. On Long Island. Now. *(Turns to face MAURICE)* It was a good idea. Here. I tell Kip. Put it in here. In this toilet,

KIP: This history.

3-YARD: *(Nodding; to MAURICE)* I mean this history. No one would know to come here and a week has gone by and the heat and the hotness?

MAURICE: *(To KIP)* You put me. In danger?

KIP: No one would know, Maurice!

MAURICE: That's why you didn't show up all week. You were waiting. To see if they. Those people you. Stole from. Had followed you. If they. Had. Followed you. *(Stunned)* Here.

KIP: Maurice! It was no danger!

(3-YARD has been glumly watching this interchange.)

3-YARD: *Breaking up!* Is so. Hard. To do. *Specially!* *(Finger in KIP's face)* For lesbos.

KIP: *(Angrily)* So let's find it! *(He starts to move restlessly about room.)*

3-YARD: Uh-uh!

(KIP halts.)

3-YARD: Organization.

KIP: *(Halting; glumly)* Sure.

(3-YARD hunches and flexes shoulders, breathes deep, postures. KIP hitches up jeans, but avoids looking at MAURICE, who is shaking his head at him.)

3-YARD: First of all. Before we start. On this. *(Looks around)* New York Public Library. We gonna settle the matter. Of the tiny little nigger. That you *(Looking at MAURICE)* brung up here. Hey?

MAURICE: Stop saying that.

3-YARD: So this nigger.

MAURICE: Stop saying that *word*!

3-YARD: So? This? Nigger?

MAURICE: He was a nice! Black. Kid.

KIP: *(Disgusted)* Jesus.

3-YARD: *(To MAURICE)* But where. Did you pop him? *(No response)* In here?

MAURICE: I don't. *Do* anything in here. Ever.

3-YARD: I get it. Might mess this— *(Gropes, indicating room)*

KIP: *(Just came to him)* Arkile!

3-YARD: *(To KIP)* Say?

KIP: Arkile.

3-YARD: That's what another word for *(Indicating room)* trash and puddle out your fanny?

MAURICE: No!

3-YARD: No who?

MAURICE: *(Angrily)* Now it's a mess! But it wasn't before. It was referenced! It was. *You* couldn't see it. You can't see anything! But it was— *(Quietly)* Organized. Beautifully. Beautifully. Organized.

(Pause, as 3-YARD lights a cigarette)

3-YARD: You know, Maurice.

MAURICE: Please don't smoke in here.

3-YARD: *(Dropping match on floor)* I *could*. Whip your mousie.

MAURICE: It's a fire hazard. Can't you see that?

3-YARD: *(Flicking ash)* Sure. I could do that. Only I don't think— *(Looks meaningfully about room)* —I gotta.

(As MAURICE looks on in dismay, 3-YARD goes to a chair, shoves off stack of clippings and sits.)

MAURICE: *(Straining against ropes; building to hysteria)* That's a collection I spent months! Tracking down, checking, and compiling. On that. Chair. That you. *(Screaming)* WANTONLY!

(3-YARD springs from chair; to MAURICE:)

3-YARD: Shut-up!

(3-YARD squeezes shut MAURICE's nose, tilting back his head.)

3-YARD: Can you breathe?

(MAURICE *flails in his chair.*)

3-YARD: Breathe through your mouth.

(MAURICE *is gasping in panic.*)

3-YARD: It's only your nose. Right? There's no noids in your mouth.

MAURICE: (*Chest heaving*) Stop it.

3-YARD: Breathe! (*Squeezes tighter*) Suck it in! (*He abruptly releases* MAURICE*'s nose.*) So that wadn't so bad. Hey? It could be worse. Right? (*Beat*) Sure.

(3-YARD *saunters away from the gasping* MAURICE.)

3-YARD: Okay. Now. Shoeboxes. Do not call cabs. And leave for Terrytown. Shoeboxes! It's a thing with them. They stay where you put it. There's a mystery here, Maurice.

(3-YARD *nods at* MAURICE, *who sighs, shakes his head, shrugs.*)

3-YARD: There is.

MAURICE: I. Yes.

3-YARD: So the thing. (*Indicating room*) About this thing. Is this. (*Pause*) All this. *Cacatz!* Is the headshot of Maurice the old queen on Avenue C she's a liberal nose and votes for the mayor. (*Points at* MAURICE) But! There's this *other* Maurice. Who stops with the scissors. And fucks off onna arkiles. And the references. And the bitches rights. (*Gripping T V tray; into* MAURICE*'s face*) And makes nasties! (*Quietly*) In her bedroom. (*Nods into* MAURICE*'s face*) And what I think. Is this *other* Maurice, who makes nasties? Took that shoebox. And put it. Somewheres. For us to find.

MAURICE: You're. Insane.

KIP: (*Intent; nodding*) That's. That's.

(To KIP, 3-YARD *makes encouraging gestures with hand.)*

KIP: That is. Fuckin. *(Again)* Brilliant.

3-YARD: *(Withdrawing)* Is what I think. This other
Maurice. A real pig this other Maurice. *Wants* us to
fuck up this *here* Maurice. With the snippers and the
People and the *Us* and the *Youse* and everything in its
place. The snatch of Maurice! Wants us to do. In. The
head of Maurice.

KIP: *(Nodding)* I'm tellin you. It's brilliant.

3-YARD: *(Nodding)* Is what I think. And so what we
gotta do. Is make that other Maurice. Tell us where
she fuckin put it. Hey? And that takes. *(Snaps fingers)*
Discipline on *this* Maurice.

KIP: Sure. Step by step. Professional.

3-YARD: *(Nodding)* Professional discipline. Right here.
(To MAURICE*)* And now.

(Pause, as MAURICE *stares at* 3-YARD *and* KIP*)*

MAURICE: Do whatever you want to me. But don't
touch anything else in tnis room. *Please.*

3-YARD: *(Nodding)* So Maurice. I want you should take
a look here. *(He goes to pile of newspapers, pulls off an old*
New York Times.*)* This, Maurice. Is disgusting. This
paper. *(Overlapping:)*

MAURICE: *(Galvinized)* That! Paper.

3-YARD: Is so old. It has a aroma. Of deadness.

MAURICE: *(Straining in his chair)* That paper. Is a
collector's item. That *Times—*

3-YARD: *(To* KIP*)* Who. I'm askin you. Who?

MAURICE: Broke the story.

3-YARD: Would read this bullshit paper anyhow?

MAURICE: Of the publication!

3-YARD: This I'm such a smart upper class jewboy so responsible the rest of you are nanderthals! Who!

MAURICE: The publication! Of the biggest story!

3-YARD: Who would read. This shit?

MAURICE: Of the publication of the Pentagon Papers it was *the* story! *the* breakthrough! of the 70s. So put it! Down.

3-YARD: I would milk off on this. And mail it back to them.

MAURICE: Down. Down. Put it down.

3-YARD: And say. Here is this dipshit paper of yours. With cum on it

KIP: And they would say. This is nonresponsible.

3-YARD: *(Heavy irony) Very* nonresponsible. But what you gonna do? When the whole world. Except for the New York *Tits!* Is some kinna fat greasy Dominican? *(Rattling* Times*)* It's very tough on these college educated.

MAURICE: *(Shaking head; hysterically) Please!* Put it—

3-YARD: Now Kip. What I want you to do. Is. *(He rips newspaper in two.)* Take this.

(MAURICE stares, wide-eyed.)

3-YARD: Down the hall. To the bat'room. *(Begins tearing newspaper in strips)* Cause there is never any tissue in there. And I want those P Rs inna next apartment? To have somethin. *(Holds out strips to* KIP*)* To wipe themselves on.

(KIP looks guiltily at MAURICE.*)*

(Hands fisted, MAURICE *convulsively throws back his head. Bellows like an animal)*

(3-YARD *quickly crosses to* MAURICE. *He stuffs the strips of newspaper into* MAURICE's *gaping mouth and holds them there.)*

3-YARD: You gettin screamy?

(MAURICE *is choking.)*

3-YARD: Gonna be quiet?

(MAURICE, *in tears from choking, desperately nods head.)*

(3-YARD *removes hand;* MAURICE *spits out paper.)*

3-YARD: Okay. So Maurice. Like I say. We gotta reach way down in there. And pull out the answer. *(Beat. He snaps fingers at* KIP, *indicating a high stack of newsprint.)* Lootenant?

(KIP, *avoiding* MAURICE's *gaze, goes reluctantly to stack. Sighs, and with one desultory swipe sends the stack sprawling over floor)*

(3-YARD *goose-steps through the debris, tearing the papers.)*

3-YARD: *(Halts; to* MAURICE) So go ahead. Call me a dago.

MAURICE: *(Exploding; through tears)* You're not! *(Quietly)* A dago.

3-YARD: Call me a dago.

MAURICE: You're worse than any. Ugly. Word.

3-YARD: Call me a dago *(No pause)* now where! Is. The shoebox?

(Beat, as MAURICE *stares through tears at debris)*

KIP: 3-Yard?

3-YARD: Grunt?

KIP: Maybe that newspaper you tore. Was worth a lotta money. Maybe she got thousands of dollars of valuable old shit in this. Maybe—

3-YARD: *(Cutting him off)* Kip?

KIP: Yessir?

3-YARD: *(Pointing at floor) Twenny push-ups!*

(KIP abruptly falls to floor and starts doing push-ups.)

3-YARD: You would question *my* tacticals? *You?* Who would be *nothin* on that street without *who?*

KIP: *(Calling out)* 3-YARD!

(3-YARD, satisfied, flexes shoulders and swaggers away, lightly tapping his fingers over the various stacks of newsprint; wanders towards bedroom.)

(KIP continues push-ups; MAURICE watches him in disbelief.)

3-YARD: *(At bedroom door)* Hey Maurice. I'm gonna organize. Your closet and your make-up kit, okay?

(MAURICE shakes his head, still staring at KIP. Exit 3-YARD into bedroom. Sounds of commotion, banging and ripping, off, during following. KIP sprawls, exhausted.)

KIP: Twenny.

MAURICE: Kip. I was. Good to you. I was— *(Intensely)* Decent! I tried to *teach* you!

KIP: You was *blabby*, Maurice. You bored me to vomit with all your noise.

MAURICE: But it's not *in* the noise! I told you. The truth. Is in the *music*, Kip. That moves through all this. This.

KIP: Fuckin this what? This arkile historydick here?

MAURICE: History, yes!

KIP: And then what happens? In this here. Music. That moves around in your yakky mouth and history?

MAURICE: *Love* happens!

(Beat. KIP moves across floor on all fours, slithers up chair and into MAURICE's face; MAURICE tries to look away.)

KIP: Old queens? Is like squish monsters like you would step on inna ocean! Always onna blab you open and close and open your hole about how fuckin much *factual!* That you had sucked up your fishfunky snatch and then go *spritz!* in my face. You hear me, Maurice? Whenever I hadda fuck you— *(Violently; into* MAURICE's *face)* I WANTED YOU SHOULD CHOKE TO DEATH AND DIE! *(He tears himself from* MAURICE, *strides to refrigerator, yanks open door. Into it, breathing hard:)* Is all you got here is eggs?

(Beat)

MAURICE: *(Staring at floor)* After the sex. When you were wasted in my sheets. You looked. Peeled. Did I ever tell you that? Like a grub without a shell. And I would tell you stories. Fill you with little pieces of this room. Little pieces. Of my dreams. Did I disgust you then? I thought it would make you. Just a little bit. Better. Just a little bit. Bigger.

(Beat; then KIP *violently slams refrigerator door.)*

KIP: I can't! Be some fuckin *hero* for you, Maurice!

*(Enter 3-*YARD *from bedroom, a leather jock strap studded with spikes spread in his hands.)*

3-YARD: You got *some* wardrobe here, Maurice. *(Flips jock over his shoulder)* But I ditn't find nothin, so—

KIP: *(Turning on 3-*YARD*)* Can we get down on this? Can we get started here?

3-YARD: *(Startled)* We started, asshole. About thirty minutes ago.

KIP: So can we move on here?

3-YARD: Did I interrupt somethin? Some dykey lesbo spat?

KIP: Fuck it. *(Turns away, grips sink, looks out window)*

3-YARD: So. Maurice.

MAURICE: *Shhhh! (Beat; hissing it:) Listen.*

3-YARD: *(Staring at* MAURICE; *to* KIP*)*: The bitch is *shushin* me now?

KIP: *(Looking down into sink)* She. Washes dishes in here. And here is also. Where you take a bath. This place. *(Looks around)* Is dinosaur New York.

3-YARD: Kip?

KIP: 3-Yard?

3-YARD: *Pay attention here!*

KIP: *(Spinning round)* I'm attention! Only this ain't workin, 3-Yard.

3-YARD: *(To* MAURICE; *exaggerated courtesy)* Excuse me? *(He approaches* KIP; *to him:)* Are we ready? For this operation? Mouth?

KIP: *(Breaking down)* What we are, 3-Yard. If we don't find that dirt? Is *cacko.* And I. *(Loud whisper)* I don't think she knows!

3-YARD: That. Kip. Is why you are a lesbo and not a commander.

KIP: It ain't workin!

3-YARD: *(Military order) Up straight!*

*(*KIP *reluctantly comes to attention.)*

3-YARD: *(Into* KIP's *face; top sergeant)* Don't you pussy out on me!

*(*KIP *blinks in fear.)*

3-YARD: Don't you spread your pink lips at me! I don't wanna see no snatch here!

*(*KIP *is at rigid attention,)*

3-YARD: I wanna see some cock and I wanna see it *now!*

KIP: Yes! *(Beat)* Sir!

3-YARD: *(Calmer)* Okay, you ready? You back in uniform?

KIP: I'm here, dominator.

3-YARD: Okay. *(Indicating radio)* That radio work?

(KIP nods. 3-YARD crosses to radio on stove, turns it on full blast: the murder scene from Berg's Lulu *bursts forth. Turns it down)*

3-YARD: *(To* MAURICE*)* You like Verdi?

MAURICE: When the music. Stops. Then you'll know.

KIP: This some kinna crazy clue, right, Maurice?

3-YARD: This is-not! A well woman here, Kip. But I guarantee you. She *will* spill her guts.

(3-YARD turns up the radio again full blast, and the Lulu *piece blares forth, filling the stage. This violent music, about midway into the following, sticks, the D J presumably snoozing; thus the few bars leading up to and including the shot repeat themselves over and over from that point to the end of the action. After turning up the radio, 3-YARD spins about, flexes shoulders, snaps his fingers at KIP, and they spring into action. For the next few moments there is utter pandemonium all over the stage. They slash into and tumble the high stacks, upend the boxes, overturn furniture, kick through the paper drifts, cut into the bundles, clear out the cabinets and empty the refrigerator of its eggs and milk. Intently, maniacally, they wad, mangle, gouge and rip, flinging bits of tabloid into the air, their movements erratic and unpredictable; the effect is of a sudden, ferocious, savaging storm.)*

(In the center of this pandemonium, MAURICE, *tied to and slumped in his chair, comprises an island of dead air and desiccation. Towards the end of this attack, this cataclysm, he looks up—just once—wide-eyed and in horror, and then his head abruptly drops, face to ceiling, over the back of the chair. His mouth is agape, his hands fisting and unfisting*

*spasmodically. He seems to be gasping for breath, then is
still. Thus, in the midst of disaster, he suddenly dies. This
need not necessarily be noticed by the audience.)*

(The fury of 3-YARD *and* KIP *spends itself at last, winds
down, depletes their reserves. They lean against the
refrigerator or they sink to their knees, breathing hard and
hoarsely, staring wildly, at exhausted rest. As one last
impulsive gesture,* 3-YARD *leaps to the radio and sends it
banging against the wall. The abrasive, discordant, ear-
splitting opera, stuck and repeating itself, is snuffed. All of
this should take no more than a minute or two of stage time,
during which the boys must have rendered the materials of
the set into an utter insensate ruin. Silence)*

3-YARD: *(Breathing hard; to* KIP*)* She even had put.
Newspaper. In her. Fuckin. Refrigerator!

KIP: *(Gasping, rising, stumbling around)* Jesus. What.
(Beat; to himself:) What did we do here?

3-YARD: Can you believe it? In her. Fridge? *(He goes to
sink, turns on tap, splashes water in face.)*

*(*KIP *pauses, turns, looks at* MAURICE*)*

KIP: *(In a whisper)* Maurice? *(He approaches* MAURICE*'s
chair. Looks at his gaping face. A little louder:)* Maurice?
(Beat) Hey.

*(*KIP *puts hand on the corpse's chest, then checks its pulse.
Meanwhile:)*

3-YARD: *(Gripping sink; out window)* I hate it! When
bitches! Put somethin in *one* place! And won't let you
move it. This! *(Beat)* I hate to fuckin hell and shit.

KIP: *(Staring down at corpse)* Jesus.

3-YARD: *(Turning round)* So okay. Maurice.

KIP: *(Dropping corpse's wrist)* She's. *(Beat; he stares.)*

3-YARD: *(To* MAURICE*)* So you had enough? *(Indicates
room)* This got to you, hey?

KIP: *(Backing away from corpse)* We flushed her! Right here. In this. Chair!

(Pause)

3-YARD: *(Stock still)* Shut up. She's fakin.

KIP: *(Staring now at 3-YARD)* We flushed the bitch! We. We shocked her fuckin heart out!

3-YARD: *(Moving nervously back and forth along sink)* She gotta pulse?

KIP: *(Hands spread; helplessly)* What we gonna do?

3-YARD: *(Sidling away)* Put your face in her face. Do you smell her breathin?

KIP: We got. No dirt. We got. A dead. *(To ceiling; loudly)* Person!

3-YARD: Shut up!

(3-YARD circles around corpse in chair as KIP crosses to sink, grips it, looks out window.)

3-YARD: *(Staring at corpse; circling)* She what?

KIP: She's dead.

3-YARD: How?

KIP: She's dead.

3-YARD: Who?

(KIP hangs head; no response.)

3-YARD: *Who?* I ast you a question! *(Halts)* This is dominator! With a question!

(Pause)

KIP: Her fuckin. Heart.

(KIP hangs head. 3-YARD stares at corpse.)

(Blackout)

END OF ACT ONE

ACT TWO

(The same. Evening)

(The stage is in that state of chaos to which it was reduced in the preceding act. Where once there were paper corridors and canyons, boxes and a careful separation of the various sorts of newsprint, a certain arrangement, now there are simply great drifts of torn and mangled paper a foot or more deep covering the floor. Refrigerator and cabinets gape, furniture is overturned and partially buried in paper. However, the downstage center apron of the stage should still be clear for action.)

(Downstage to the side there is now an addition: a green plastic garbage bag tied at one end, humped, and containing MAURICE's body. Radio lies where it was flung.)

(3-YARD and KIP are now searching the debris, but this time with something in the way of method. On all fours they root among the drifts, often crossing one another's path. Often, as they burrow, we lose sight of their faces. They are actuated now by a palpable desperation prickling on the skin. Their interchange is rapid-fire and overlapping.)

KIP: We're gonna die.

3-YARD: Shut your hole.

KIP: The whole world of New York out there?

3-YARD: So?

KIP: Gonna dick us with shotguns and fuck us dead.

3-YARD: Where is that suckin box?

KIP: You said it would be good here to hide it here.

3-YARD: But I *ditn't*! Know that *you*!

KIP: Who?

3-YARD: Had no control on your bitch.

KIP: She ditn't *know* where it was, 3-Yard.

3-YARD: She knows. *(Indicating garbage bag)* In that fuckin garbage bag?

KIP: You bashed her heart and she ditn't! Even!

3-YARD: Is a dead! bitch! that could tell us where! she hid the dirt.

KIP: Where inna hell. We gonna *put* her?

3-YARD: You let me worry, okay? Just find the shoebox we wait til Gooey shows up. We drive her down we stick her inna river.

KIP: *What* river? The East? Or the Harlem? Or what?

3-YARD: What the fuckin fuck! Does it give a shit. Whose shitty river! We put her in?

KIP: *(Meaning* MAURICE*)* She would hate it. To be inna river.

3-YARD: So we don't *put* her inna river. Hey? So we could drive out to City Island we could eat! Inna lobster restaurant! And stick her! Inna Long Island Sound. Okay?

KIP: Even to put her. In that bag. She hated it when! *(Pause)* When you put anything over her face.

3-YARD: *(Pausing also and staring)* Who?

KIP: Even in that bag. She would hate it. And then. To drop her. In the water. Where it's dark for her. And no air. She just would. *(He shakes his head and stares at bag.)*

(3-YARD stares, and then crawls towards KIP.*)*

3-YARD: *(Nodding)* Sure. She would wet her panties. *(Into* KIP's *face)* If the bitch! Could breathe. But! She has sucked her last weewee and you! Are some kinna. Hamburger! And you! Better! And.

KIP: *(Exploding) I don't take your orders no more!*

*(3-*YARD *and* KIP *are nose-to-nose on all fours.)*

3-YARD: Say?

KIP: You don't treat me like toilet paper. No. More!

3-YARD: You Irish nigger fuckin lesbo suck.

KIP: You don't! Dominator me! No. More! Because. *(Raises hand from floor, points finger under* 3-YARD's *nose)* We are in this thing. Because you. Come in here. You set this up. And did her. To death. On *your* orders! And that's. What I'll say.

3-YARD: You'll say that.

KIP: This was *your* sack of heat!

3-YARD: You gonna tell this. To who?

KIP: And that's what I know. So you—

3-YARD: Who to? You gonna tell this?

KIP: Better treat me with some idea. Of this. And—

3-YARD: *Who!*

*(*KIP *looks away.)*

3-YARD: To some kinna police? That *I*. Made *you*. Monkey here. Around. So her cardiacs! Jumped through her phobics! And she cacks. So this. You're gonna say? Fine. *(Sits back on haunches, nods maniacally)* Sounds good.

KIP: *(Desperately)* I told you I said back off! Twice I told you!

3-YARD: I seem to member that *you*. Got screamy. With her. Over how you. Did I hear? From the bedroom?

KIP: Twice! Maybe even. Three or four times!

3-YARD: About how these queens. Like her. Was sea pussies or ocean shit *(No pause) some* kinna weird you was screamin in her hole! It was insults. And then! She died.

KIP: That! Is a fuckin story.

3-YARD: *(Abrupt)* You think that nigger took the box?

(3-YARD and KIP stare at one another.)

KIP: Jesus.

(3-YARD and KIP dive into debris, again without a coordinated plan.)

(Much desperate rummaging)

(Finally 3-YARD springs to his feet, marches to an overturned chair, takes it downstage and clears a space with his boot, then firmly sets down chair and sits, holding head in hands.)

3-YARD: Okay. Now.

KIP: *(Looking up)* The fuck is this are you?

3-YARD: Organization. Now. Gooey is comin here.

KIP: So?

3-YARD: With a Hertz-a-car. So much for this funeral. Of Maurice. Okay. Now. The problem is.

KIP: The problem? Is fuckin. Pretty clear here, 3-Yard.

3-YARD: Is what. Do I tell Gooey?

KIP: So who gives a cocksuck what we say to *her*?

3-YARD: It's. Very understated. I think, Kip. Maybe that when she gets here? You just keep lookin. And don't say nothin. I will do for Gooey.

KIP: *(Consternation)* What's? What's?

3-YARD: Just keep your mouth! Shut!

KIP: *I don't take your orders! (Pause. He stands, stumbles through debris, approaching* 3-YARD.*)* You take off my own bitch and now you sit here. And whine to me. About *your* bitch. Who is still *out* here. With her *tits!* And I.

3-YARD: Don't push me, Kip.

KIP: I got *no* apartment. No place to go if I *need* a place. I got. *No* steady mark. I got people lookin to hell me cause of this dirt you stole. I got no. *Back up.* You get me?

3-YARD: Just do. The thing. I say. Okay?

KIP: *(Indicating bag)* That old number you took off? That old-number was. *(Gropes)* A lady! And. And you!

3-YARD: Pushin me? You are pushin me?

KIP: Sit here! And whack off! About this jewey Gooey snatch who.

3-YARD: I just don't wanna upset her, that's all!

KIP: Oh. You don't wanna. Upset her.

3-YARD: She's a nervous. Constitution.

KIP: She's a big whore! And I'm suppose to pussyfloat. Around this whore! After you! Flushed the heart. Outa my. *(Pause, as he looks at bag. Quietly, almost affectionately)* Best. Mark. *(He stares at bag.)*

(There is a knock at the door. 3-YARD *springs to his feet. Into* KIP's *ear, as* KIP *muses, unconscious of knocking:)*

3-YARD: Do what I say! Keep shut and find! That *box!*

(3-YARD pushes KIP, *who shakes him off. Then* KIP *begins searching, despairingly, desultorily, then in earnest.)*

(3-YARD stumbles to door; opens it.)

(Enter GOOEY.*)*

(Without a word to GOOEY, 3-YARD *gives the landing a quick once-over, closes door, and then begins searching intently.)*

GOOEY: *(Chewing gum, looking around room)* This. Is a scandal. *(To* 3-YARD*)* Honey? *(No response)* Sweetness? *(Same)* How. Does Maurice live here? *(Same)* Anyway. They should fix that street door. *(No response)* Honey? *(Same)* Lovebucket? You could get raped up here. *(Looks from one preoccupied boy to the other; shrugs, moves downstage; to* 3-YARD*:)* The car's downstairs. Around the block. That school with the mural looks like Fidel Castro on poppers? *(No pause)* it's so fuckin hot I could die. *(Spies empty chair; sits in it; watches boys. Dizzy and nattering, chewing gum:)* The Hertz people? Would not believe it was my credit card. Well. I said. What do I look like some kinna China woman? *(Pause)* I borrowed that card off a dyke on East 85th that! Is a neighborhood. Yesterday I went up there it's a dyke in a brownstone. Sometimes I do her hair. The card? The license? It's a New Jersey license you would be *stupid!* To question this. She. The dyke. Said it's good for forty-eight hours at the least. So finally. Anyhow. They accepted it. At Hertz. *(Silence)* So. We drive out to the Island, deliver, park the fuckin Datsun, and take the train home. I am sick! Of those putzes! At Hertz. Next time? I'll use Avis or I'll go to my local Cuban.

(Still no response from 3-YARD *and* KIP, *who continue search.* GOOEY *takes a beat, then picks up a magazine from floor, casually leafing through it. Looks up at* 3-YARD*)*

GOOEY: Okay, honey bee? *(No response; she reads magazine)* God. This *Cosmo* is so *old.* Here's this ad for that Maybelline that bombed? Do you believe that a corporation as rich as she is? As rich. As *Maybelline?* Would come up with the color of dog shit and call it "Mahogany" with eyeliner to match? I said. When I saw it. When it first came out. This was *years* ago.

I said. You put this on your nails. You put it for chrissakes on your *face*? And they won't serve you in the better restaurants. *(Beat; still leafing)* Lover love? *(Looks up sharply at* 3-YARD*)* Honey? *(Beat)* So what's this?

3-YARD: *(Intent on search)* What's who?

GOOEY: This. All this. That's. *(Looks around)* Transpiring.

*(*3-YARD *does not respond;* GOOEY *leafs some more through magazine.)*

GOOEY: Fucking god. Herbal shampoos. They were very drying and made your hair? smell like crab grass. *(Without looking up)* Honey? What's in the bag?

*(*3-YARD *still does not respond, but he does accelerate search.)*

KIP: *(To* GOOEY; *intent on search; over his shoulder)* Maurice.

*(*GOOEY *reacts by not chewing.* 3-YARD *throws* KIP *a nasty look.)*

(Beat)

GOOEY: *(Addressing bag)* So Maurice what are we playing here? *(Chewing gum; leafing)* It's what, what is it? "Take Out This Garbage"? Is that what we're playing? *(Indicating* 3-YARD *and* KIP*)* These big dirty garbagemen gonna haul your trash down to the street you know bumpity-bump down the stairs?

(To 3-YARD, *passing by:)*

GOOEY: Could be a hoot, right? *(To the bag)* So Maurice. What are you gonna do when the garbage truck comes? You gonna wait til the sanitation men throw you on the truck and then what? Jump out stark naked, right? Like: "TA-DA!" Is that the movie?

(To 3-YARD, *passing the other way:)*

GOOEY: "TA-DA!" *(To the bag)* It's good I like it.

(3-YARD crosses to bedroom doorway.)

3-YARD: *(To* KIP*)* I'm gonna look in here. One more time. *(He exits into bedroom.)*

GOOEY: *(Leafing; to* KIP*)* He gonna what?

KIP: *(Impatiently; passing by, intent)* Maurice is dead we lost the dirt here in this.

(Long pause)

*(*GOOEY *stares into audience. Drops magazine. Stands, moves downstage center. Facing audience:)*

GOOEY: *(Calling sweetly)* 3-Yard? Honey babe?

3-YARD: *(Offstage)* Not now, Gooey.

(Beat)

GOOEY: *(Low; hard)* Fuckin get your ass. *(Beat) In— (An immense and shattering bellow)* HEEEEEEERE! *(Long and drawn out, her bellow strafes the room like a machine gun, as she slowly rotates her head from one side to the other.)*

*(*KIP *halts, stunned by the force of her lung power, and watches.)*

(3-YARD pops into bedroom doorway.)

3-YARD: *(Placating)* Okay. Okay. Okay.

*(*GOOEY *jabs her finger at spot on floor beside her.)*

(3-YARD hesitates; GOOEY *jabs again with finger)*

(3-YARD stumbles downstage, not knowing what to do with his hands.)

3-YARD: *(As if handling dynamite)* Look. Gooey. It's been. A taxation here. Of my nerves. So. You gotta be. You get me?

(Beat, as GOOEY *stares at 3-YARD)*

3-YARD: The thing is, there was this nigger with the New York Mets and we ain't too sure. It still could *be* here, but. *(To* KIP*)* Hey. It still could be here? *(No response; to* GOOEY*)* Sure. So it will take awhile because this. I mean. *(Gestures at bag, helplessly)* She died.

(Beat)

GOOEY: *(Deadpan)* She died.

3-YARD: *(Nodding)* She died.

GOOEY: *(A little higher)* She died?

3-YARD: *(Same)* Yeah. She just. Died.

*(*GOOEY *glares coldly into* 3-YARD*'s face.)*

3-YARD: *(Placating; raising hands)* We ditn't touch her. *(To* KIP*)* Did we touch her?

*(*KIP *slowly shakes head.)*

*(*GOOEY *turns abruptly away from* 3-YARD *and moves downstage. Facing audience, she snaps her fingers and wriggles them.)*

3-YARD: *(In response to* GOOEY*'s gesture)* Okay. Right. So Kip. You came here today?

KIP: *(Low, deliberate, hateful)* Yeah.

3-YARD: *(Talking as much to* GOOEY*'s back as to* KIP*)* And Maurice was here. Like always with the old papers and shit. You know, she likes to clipper and snip it's a thing with her. *(Looks hopefully at* KIP*; no response)* It's a thing and you had put the shoebox. With the dirt in it. Under the sink. Only it wadn't there and Maurice? Plays her games with you. Maybe she gave it to some nigger kid she had up here maybe not but anyhow. When I get here. I gotta take. Control.

KIP: *(Nodding maliciously; indicating* GOOEY*)* Yeah right. You got lots of control.

3-YARD: *(Angrily)* So I come in here! Thinkin I will find! The old queen snippin her way! Through the Sunday *Times!* And my lootenant! With the shoebox in his hands! But what! It really! *IS!*

KIP: You would call *me* a female lesbo?

(GOOEY is staring glumly into audience.)

(KIP has confronted 3-YARD; they are nose to nose.)

3-YARD: *(Defensive; angry)* No control! No dirt! This dead queen!

KIP: Oh? *(Goosenecks)* Oh? Who's fault was this?

3-YARD: This is what I'm sayin.

KIP: This was you! Who shocked the shit. Outa my! *(Goosenecks wildly)* And now!

3-YARD: This is exactly! What I'm sayin.

KIP: You stand here!

3-YARD: And it's clear. To every person.

KIP: You stand right! Here!

3-YARD: To every person with legs and eyes! That.

KIP: With pussy! All over! Your face!

(3-YARD and KIP abruptly part, pace, return; nose to nose. GOOEY still looks glumly at audience.)

3-YARD: You are nothin! Without dominator.

KIP: *(Laughing harshly)* Dominator?

3-YARD: *(Goosenecks)* Your equipment? Is like. You gotta have a search warrant.

KIP: But *you?* Use your tongue!

3-YARD: *(Same)* Hung like a pencil!

KIP: You could use it maybe. On *me!*

3-YARD: *(Staring)* I suspected this! All day!

KIP: Yeah? *(Double take)* You *what*?

3-YARD: *(Grasping himself)* That you would *love* it I give you a treatment!

KIP: That is a fuckin horseshit! I seen you smilin at me!

3-YARD: Who?

KIP: When you was ballin *(Indicating* GOOEY*)* this bitch for Maurice I seen you smilin at me!

3-YARD: This! Is fantasyland. I *never*!

KIP: You can't get off out a guy watchin you!

3-YARD: *(Jabbing fist under* KIP's *nose)* You eat that!

KIP: No!

3-YARD: You eat what you said!

KIP: *(Pushing* 3-YARD *away)* You! Are nothin. Without guys. *(Pause; low and predatory)* You always need me, 3-Yard. Like you need the amateurs and the losers inna bars. *You!* Wanna get *us*! Hot! For *you*!

(3-YARD backs away; KIP *stalks him.)*

KIP: If this world. Was only girls. You would die. And be fuckless. *(His finger is rigid in* 3-YARD's *face.)*

(Pause)

3-YARD: *(Breaking away; to* GOOEY*)* You hear this?

(GOOEY continues staring glumly at audience.)

3-YARD: This shit. You hear it? You hear this insults? See what I had here? *(No response; to* KIP*)* You! Are court martial. You are no lootenant to me.

KIP: That's great.

3-YARD: That's good.

(3-YARD and KIP *begin passing back and forth; as they pass one another:)*

KIP: It's what I said.

3-YARD: I court martial your ass.

KIP: Lootenant to what?

3-YARD: I hadda do it.

KIP: To a pussy's pussy? This is no kinna status. *(Indicating* GOOEY*)* Of a Jew beautician? From Flushing?

3-YARD: It was a decision I hadda make it!

*(*KIP *abruptly turns, kicks through debris, grips sink, looking out window)*

KIP: *(In a low distinct voice)* We. Are gonna. Die. *(Pause)*

3-YARD: *(Nervously; to* GOOEY*)* So. You see what I had here?

*(*GOOEY *has by now sat down again and is leafing through a magazine.)*

3-YARD: I mean. I took it all down. *(Holds up palm, reads)* It says. This Irishwoman. Has been fired. From the service. Of dominator. She has shown fear under fire and she's a lesbo on toppa that. See?

*(*3-YARD *flashes palm in* GOOEY*'s direction; she doesn't look up.)*

3-YARD: We got a record of this. For our files. *(Beat; lowers palm)* So that's. Taken care of. *(He looks furtively at* GOOEY*.)*

GOOEY: *(Snapping her fingers)* Come here.

*(*3-YARD *stumbles through debris to stand next to* GOOEY*'s chair. Looking at his crotch, which is eye-level:)*

GOOEY: What am I suppose to do, talk Yiddish to your foreskin?

*(*3-YARD *hastily crouches by chair.)*

GOOEY: Thank you. *(Leafing through magazine)* So. A human being? With testicles? Is mainly mouth. Hmmm?

3-YARD: Gooey—

GOOEY: And you know! There's more mouth. In New York City? Than there are Jews in Israel.

(Explosively, with the back of her hand, GOOEY lashes out, catching 3-YARD full in the face. He reels and spins away. She follows him, systematically slapping him about the head and shoulders as he tries to duck away.)

(Finally 3 YARD collapses, humiliated, in the center of room, his head between his knees.)

(GOOEY stands over 3 YARD, breathing hard. Casually she begins to examine her nails.)

(KIP has been watching all this, stunned.)

GOOEY: Now you know, 3-Yard. That I set this thing up. And I can pull the plug on you. Anytime.

KIP: *(To GOOEY) You* set it up?

GOOEY: *(To 3-YARD)* And I am not conversing. *(Indicating KIP)* With this lootenant you got *(No pause)* he called me a beautician. Hey? 3-Yard?

3-YARD: *(Muffled; unmoving)* You shouldn't do this. To me.

GOOEY: You fucked up, honey, and I want you to bleed a little, okay?

3-YARD: *(Looking up; then hiding head)* Not in front of! Nobody else.

GOOEY: We are a little short of time, 3-Yard, and I can't wait til we get home. For this. And I want you to bleed. Just a little. For your bitch. 3-Yard? *(Beat)* I have sat. And watched you. In numerous bars and teques. Like a good little bitch. Ever since we met. At that tea dance? For that leatherhead photographer you were shvantzing? Who had promised you a centerfold in *Playguy* and *(Building to rage)* the only spread you ever saw WAS WHEN HE SPREAD THE TATTOOES ON HIS TUSH??? Have sat and watched you and waited. Til we got home. To give you the word. About who was dippable. Who was usable. And who was not. Hey?

3-YARD: *(Muffled)* I know, Gooey.

GOOEY: And now, see. I'm telling you. To get up. And bleed.

3-YARD: *(Petulant)* No.

GOOEY: *(Bending down; sweetly)* Baby, I want you to get up.

3-YARD: *(Same)* I am not gettin up!

GOOEY: *(Same)* I want you to get up and stand here like a man. Because you have not been a man. For weeks. Almost.

3-YARD: *(Quiet, hurt)* No. I won't.

GOOEY: It has been very distressing.

3-YARD: *(Same)* You shouldn't'a done it.

GOOEY: I am distressed and I might just as soon? 3-Yard? Have bought a package of franks to steam on the stove for all. The good? You been. To me.

3-YARD: I been nervous!

(KIP laughs harshly.)

(GOOEY straightens up.)

GOOEY: *(To 3-YARD)* I want you. To tell your lootenant. Not to laugh anymore and to suck his fingers. Okay? I want you to tell him.

3-YARD: *(Still muffled)* Suck your fingers, Kip!

KIP: I don't take orders from you, 3-Yard.

(GOOEY *stares hard at* KIP. *She looks back down at* 3-YARD.)

GOOEY: *(Harder now)* I want you on your feet, baby. Right now. Cause I don't wanna talk to this *(Indicating* KIP*)* lunchbucket.

KIP: *(To her back)* Say who?

GOOEY: *(To* 3-YARD; *again indicating* KIP; *harder still:)* This baba! Ganoush!

(3-YARD *climbs slowly to his feet. He stands there flushed, humiliated, scared.)*

3-YARD: What we gonna do? Gooey?

GOOEY: *(As if to a child)* That's what I gotta consider. So you take this *(Indicating chair)* over there. *(Indicating cleared space further downstage center)* Where I can be comfortable and think it out. Okay?

(3-YARD *nods and moves chair where indicated.* GOOEY *casually sits in it, crossing her legs.* 3-YARD *squats by chair, looking at her eagerly.* KIP *watches all this contemptuously.* 3-YARD *and* GOOEY *play a rapid nodding game throughout the following:)*

GOOEY: *(To* 3-YARD*)* Now. You know when I set this deal up it was very touchy.

(3-YARD *nods.)*

GOOEY: I hadda have partners. *(Again)* Cause what we did, we went and emptied both our large. And our small. Intestines? All over syndicate. Get me?

3-YARD: *(Holding up palm)* It's written right here. That this was a very risky operation.

GOOEY: Right. And the only reason. We got this opportunity? Was because we was disconnected, available, and could deep-six and deliver the merchandise *(No pause)* you takin this down?

3-YARD: *(Nodding, tapping palm)* Engraved.

GOOEY: So basically we are unprotected here. And the partners on Long Island, if we don't deliver today? Are gonna lose control of their bladders and send *finger-paintings! Of our faces! To the syndicate!* So what I wanna know. *(Smiling sweetly, looking about room)* Is what happened in here?

3-YARD: Okay. You member you told me that Maurice. Might be a problem?

GOOEY: *(Nodding)* Yes. I mentioned to you. That Maurice. Could play games.

3-YARD: That she could find the box and play it for a sex thing?

GOOEY: I said it was a risk. I mentioned this.

3-YARD: Well see. That's what happened. Kip gets here and the shoebox. Is gone. From where he put it.

(GOOEY nods coldly.)

3-YARD: Under the sink. *(Again)* So. We gotta drag it outa Maurice.

GOOEY: You told her like I said, right? That she's this big intellectual over here and in there *(Indicating bedroom)* in bed? she's a pigdog *(No pause)* you told her this? That we could unlock her nervous system? And fuck her. *In her card catalogue?*

(3-YARD nods.)

KIP: *(Shaking head in contempt)* The big brilliant dominator.

GOOEY: *(To 3-YARD; nodding)* And it got to her?

3-YARD: *(Nodding)* She said I was. Bazoo.

GOOEY: But it got to her?

3-YARD: Yeah. It registered.

GOOEY: And so then?

3-YARD: She wouldn't tell us. So I did what you said. I went after this— *(Indicating room)* This—

GOOEY: *(Nodding)* A tightass like Maurice. Would be very upset. If you touch one thing.

3-YARD: So. We did that.

KIP: *(Contemptuously, staring at 3-YARD)* The pussy's pussy.

3-YARD: *(Ignoring KIP, but bridling at his words)* So. We. Did this. To this. Here. In this.

GOOEY: *(Nodding)* 3-Yard. What I told you. Was. I mean. This was always a mess in here I was shocked at Maurice. But now. *(Looking about)* It's like. The Bronx. Got gentrified. With a Cuisinart. So what. *(Hard)* Happened here?

3-YARD: *(Helplessly)* She wouldn't spit it up!

KIP: Pussy whippy pussy whip.

(GOOEY stops nodding; beat; rapidly:)

GOOEY: *(To 3-YARD, indicating KIP)* Tell him to shut up.

3-YARD: Shut up, Kip.

KIP: Fuck you, 3-Yard.

GOOEY: *(To 3-YARD)* I want him to shut up.

3-YARD: Shut up, Kip.

KIP: Fuck you, 3-Yard.

GOOEY: *(Calm; to 3-YARD)* Tell him to shut up.

3-YARD: *(To KIP)* Shut up, Kip.

KIP: Fuck you too, Gooey.

GOOEY: *(Same)* Tell him to shut up.

3-YARD: Shut up, Kip.

KIP: Fuck you 3-Yard.

GOOEY: Tell him he's dead! *(Beat)* A dead whoor.
Without. Me. *(Beat)*

(KIP turns away, grips sink, looking into it.)

3-YARD: *(To GOOEY)* So. That's how. It happened.

GOOEY: In other words. You mishandled. My
instructions?

3-YARD: No. See.

GOOEY: Because what I said. Was threaten her library. I
did not say. To drop a bomb in here. Did I?

(3-YARD shakes his head guiltily.)

GOOEY: So you're this crude. And stupid. Asshole.
Okay?

(3-YARD nods reluctantly.)

GOOEY: Show me some pink.

3-YARD: Gooey, come on. Hey.

GOOEY: I want you to pink out for me. For your very
own bitch. Right here. And now. *(Beat)* I mean. There's
a whole new order comin here. This jungle here? Is
not like it was for your Italian mau-mau forefathers.
I see here. A whole new vision. Of bitches. All over
New York. And maybe even the boroughs. In tight
jeans with our titties spilling out? Gripping pool sticks.
While the guys? *(Into his face)* Squat!

(3-YARD closes his eyes.)

GOOEY: On the barstools. Wearing very. Short. Leashes.
(Beat) Now. Show me some pink.

(3-YARD despairingly shakes head.)

GOOEY: Show me. Some pink.

(3-YARD same.)

GOOEY: Show me.

(3-YARD *same*)

GOOEY: *(Coyly)* 3-Yard?

(3-YARD *hangs head.*)

GOOEY: Show pink to your bitch.

(3-YARD *slowly raises his head, eyes closed, and distends the full length of his tongue.*)

(GOOEY *bends, examining it.*)

GOOEY: *(Nodding; pronouncing every syllable)* Very. Interesting. *(Quick and casual; indicating garbage bag)* How did Maurice get in the bag?

3-YARD: *(Withdrawing tongue; hangdog)* We thought. Maybe. We would drive her to. Say. The Harlem River.

GOOEY: Instead of the beach? You know at Riis Park she could get herself a tan. *(Exploding) I'm asking you! Why! She's dead in that bag!*

3-YARD: *(Quickly)* She had this phobic!

(GOOEY *stares.*)

GOOEY: She hadda *what*?

KIP: *(Spinning round)* She hadda heart condition! *(Turns, grips sink again)* She was sick in her heart.

3-YARD: *(To* GOOEY; *nodding)* Cardiacs and shit.

(Beat)

GOOEY: And because you two. Lunched out. Souvlaki? Sandwiches? Bombed the woman's house. With the crudeness and the clumsiness? She has a heart attack. And checks out. With the secret. Of the shoebox. In her luggage?

(GOOEY *looks heavily inquisitive at* 3-YARD; *he nods guiltily.*)

Perfect. *(Beat)* Say it.

3-YARD: I'm a asshole.

KIP: *(Spinning round; to* 3-YARD*)* You're a pussy mouth!

3-YARD: Stay outa this!

GOOEY: *(Snapping her fingers; to* 3-YARD, *indicating* KIP*)* Tell your lootenant. That everything I have said here? Goes for him too. Only *HE!* I'm told. *(Beat)* Is hung like a Paper-Mate.

*(*KIP *sullenly turns back to look in sink.)*

GOOEY: *(To* 3-YARD*)* So. How bad did you hurt Maurice?

3-YARD: *(Throwing up his hands)* I ditn't touch her!

*(*GOOEY *looks hard at* 3-YARD.*)*

3-YARD: Except I futz her around a little. *(Pointing at* KIP*)* Only he? That one? Kicks her in her uterus!

KIP: *(Not turning round)* By *your* orders!

3-YARD: *(Springing up; approaching* KIP*)* That is a cockface lie!

KIP: *(Spinning round; meeting* 3-YARD*)* You choked *my* bitch and hurt her mouth!

*(*3-YARD *and* KIP *are nose to nose.)*

*(*GOOEY *stares glumly at audience.)*

3-YARD: She gotta have a bruise! On her vagina! So big!

KIP: A cut on her lip you could drive a *truck!*

3-YARD: Which prob'ly! Fucked her guts! To hemmorage!

KIP: She gotta need stitches! From her gums! *All* across her cheek!

3-YARD: And bleed! All over! Her cardiacs!

GOOEY: *(Hard and sharp; still looking at audience)* 3-Yard!

*(*3-YARD *and* KIP *both look at* GOOEY.*)*

3-YARD: Say?

(GOOEY snaps her fingers, indicating spot next to chair. 3-YARD, sheepish, breaks from KIP and moves to spot indicated; KIP watches contemptuously and returns to grip sink again.)

GOOEY: *(Calmly; to 3-YARD)* So the thing here. That burns to be answered. Is. How soon. Did she make her exit. After you scrambled her eggs?

3-YARD: It was. Months later. Like when she cacked? It was after we tied her. To the chair.

GOOEY: *(Deadly calm)* You tied her. To a chair?

3-YARD: Not a finger of my hand! *(Indicating KIP)* Or this lesbo over here. *(Throws up hands)* Was laid on her. She just. *(Pause)* Died. *(Indicating GOOEY's chair)* In that chair.

(GOOEY looks down at chair.)

GOOEY: Okay. *(Springs to her feet)* Get rid! Of the chair. Find me another.

(3-YARD hastily drags chair away, flings it into debris.)

3-YARD: Kip, get her another chair.

KIP: *(Turning round; to 3-YARD)* Eat my feet.

3-YARD: I said!

(GOOEY snaps fingers; 3-YARD falls silent.)

(GOOEY and KIP stare at each other, GOOEY cold and composed, KIP nervously gripping sink behind him.)

KIP: There's a rocker thing. In Maurice's bedroom.

3-YARD: *(Nodding)* Right. *(He exits into bedroom and re-enters with a rocking chair, dragging it through debris, placing it center stage in downstage cleared area.)*

(During this business, KIP darts wary glances at GOOEY, who, hands on hips, approaches him, stares him up and down, appraisingly, and then saunters away, sitting in the rocker provided.)

(3-YARD *crouches by rocker.*)

GOOEY: (*Rocking languidly; to* 3-YARD) So Maurice. Popped off. *After* you made breakfast. With her face and her belly?

3-YARD: Long time after. When we was. (*He gestures about room.*)

GOOEY: Bombing the jesus christ. Out of her apartment?

(3-YARD *nods guiltily.*)

GOOEY: (*Shrugging*) Then Maurice is not a problem.

KIP: (*At sink, watching; low and disdainful*) Not a problem.

3-YARD: (*Watching* GOOEY) No?

GOOEY: (*To* 3-YARD; *putting a cigarette between her lips*) No.

KIP: It's a fire hazard in here, Gooey.

(3-YARD *lights* GOOEY'*s cigarette; they ignore* KIP.)

(KIP *then strides to middle of room; he pauses by bag, hitches up jeans, points at bag; to* GOOEY:)

KIP: So what. Are we gonna do. *With the body?* (*Plucks at his basket, very macho*) Is what I wanna know.

GOOEY: (*Amusedly watching* KIP; *exhaling smoke*) Well. You could. First off. Shake her outa that bag. And into her bed. So it looks like. She died in her sleep.

KIP: She got. *Marks!* On her body.

GOOEY: I don't think. A futz in her teeth. Or a poke from your tiny tennies? Is gonna look like. Murder.

(*Pause, as* KIP *ponders this*)

GOOEY: (*Shrugging*) Or leave her in the bag. Eventually the cops will come in here, cut her open, and say—

KIP: (*Overlapping; staring at bag*) Cut her open?

GOOEY: She was this old fag. Who got all hotted up. In some kinna comedy session? And expired with a heart attack. Now you could. Maybe. Open the bag and throw in a popper *(No pause)* but Maurice! Is not. A problem.

KIP: We just. Gonna leave her here?

(3-YARD rises, paces, raises finger.)

3-YARD: That! Is brain cells.

(GOOEY shrugs, rocking and smoking.)

(KIP looks up from bag, approaches GOOEY; poses, very macho, plucking at his basket again.)

KIP: *(To GOOEY)* Okay. Okay. I'm gonna *assume.* For the moment. That this. Is computer precision. Thinking. Just for now. *(Plucking)* But the question. Upper level on *my* mind. Is this.

GOOEY: *(Indicating KIP's crotch)* You got crabs is what you got?

KIP: *(Pauses; stops plucking)* Huh?

GOOEY: Why are you playing with yourself?

(KIP stares at GOOEY.)

GOOEY: I mean, with a Puerto Rican you could understand it. I mean. Puerto Ricans? Cultivate crabs. In window boxes. In their apartments. But you! Got no excuse.

(KIP flexes, looks defiantly at GOOEY.)

KIP: Who?

GOOEY: You.

KIP: Who?

GOOEY: You.

3-YARD: He thinks, Gooey. That he is on equal categories. With us. *(Thumbs in belt, slouching easily)* He thinks he is showin. Cock.

GOOEY: *(To 3-YARD; sharply)* I have seen. 3-Yard. Very little of *that*. Lately.

3-YARD: *(Nervously; dropping pose)* I. Gooey. Will make you. Cross-eyed. When all this is over. Hey? Cross-eyed.

KIP: *(To GOOEY; indicating 3-YARD)* He's a loser.

(3-YARD moves towards KIP menacingly; GOOEY snaps her fingers and 3-YARD withdraws.)

GOOEY: *(Appraising KIP)* Whereupon?

KIP: You what?

GOOEY: Whereupon you. Are not? A loser?

KIP: *(Thumbs in belt, slouching self-consciously)* You know. What I'm sayin. Cause upper level here! Is the question. Of who. Is next in command here.

(GOOEY throws cigarette on floor; KIP looks, hastily stamps it out.)

3-YARD: Like I said, Gooey. Two inches. At the most? Maybe three.

GOOEY: So the main problem. Is this mystery shoebox. Did somebody check out the bedroom?

3-YARD: I checked it out.

GOOEY: *(To KIP)* And did you double-check him?

(KIP sullenly shakes his head.)

GOOEY: You thought maybe. It was better not to?

(KIP stands there, his mouth working in anger, then he strides through debris into bedroom. We hear, off, a great banging about.)

(GOOEY *stands, moves quickly to side of stage, snaps her fingers at* 3-YARD, *who moves to her side.*)

GOOEY: We drive Kip to where is he livin?

3-YARD: He what?

GOOEY: *(Hissing) Where's Kip at this week?*

3-YARD: That bartender's. On Rivington.

GOOEY: *(Begin pacing; fast:)* Okay. We drop him off so's he can get his gear he knows we can't stay in town. We drive on to get our gear tell him we'll pick him up where? Rivington and what?

3-YARD: Gooey? Be simple.

GOOEY: So we drive on pick up our gear I make a little phone call, get me?

(3-YARD *shakes his head in confusion;* GOOEY *grabs him by neck.*)

GOOEY: Look! Pretty soon those small-change on Long Island gonna throw us to the syndicate. So what I'm gonna do, is tell Long Island that Kip. Offed Maurice. And ran off with the merchandise. They can throw *Kip*. To the syndicate.

3-YARD: My own. Lootenant?

GOOEY: We need a fall guy! Somebody they can jump on. *(Releases* 3-YARD; *pacing again)* It will take a lotta heat off us and we can get the hell outa New York. A body, that's all we need.

3-YARD: A body?

GOOEY: A coupla legs, a few arms, some face. Kip. Has. A body! So Rivington and what?

3-YARD: You gonna have him. Picked off?

GOOEY: After I make the phone call? We drive on to D C go to sleep for awhile. Rivington and what?

3-YARD: You can't. Do this.

(GOOEY *snaps fingers in* 3-YARD's *face.*)

GOOEY: Any *body*! Will do, 3-Yard. Rivington and what?

3-YARD: It's. I dunno. It's middle of the block. Between the fuckin Bowery. And Chrystie.

GOOEY: *(Nodding)* So Rivington and the fuckin Bowery.

3-YARD: Or Chrystie and Eldridge. Maybe he's closer to Eldridge.

GOOEY: *So which is it?*

3-YARD: I think he's closer to Eldridge.

GOOEY: *(Pacing away)* Jee-*sus*!

3-YARD: The Bowery, the fuckin Bowery!

(GOOEY *paces back to* 3-YARD; *her nose to his.*)

GOOEY: We get mixed up on the precise and exact corner? And D C is not far enough. We will have to move. To *Poland*!

3-YARD: I said it was the fuckin Bowery!

GOOEY: Okay. I let it be known. There is a warm body. In full and final payment for this. *(Looks around room; gestures helplessly)* This *shtup-a-thon*! At Rivington and the fuckin Bowery. They'll go for his ass while we get outa town.

3-YARD: But Gooey. Maybe. *(Gesturing around room)* It's *here.*

GOOEY: We will certainly make an effort. But much time? We haven't got. *(She crosses back to rocker, sits; composes herself; to* 3-YARD.) Now get to work.

(3-YARD *hastily drops to his knees and begins rummaging through debris.*)

(KIP *emerges from bedroom.*)

KIP: *(Pointing decisively at floor; to* GOOEY*)* It's in here. Somewhere. In here.

GOOEY: *(Calmly lighting a cigarette)* It always pays to check double. *(Exhaling and rocking)* Now. Was there not. A suggestion. Earlier today. Of a negro?

KIP: *(At a loss)* A who?

GOOEY: Did I not hear of a negro mentioned here?

3-YARD: *(Looking up)* Oh yeah. That nigger kid Maurice turned in this.

KIP: *(To* 3-YARD*)* Okay. Okay. *(Looks around room; desperately authoritative)* If we don't find you know. The shoebox? We will go down. To Tomkins. We will grill his ass.

3-YARD: Right!

*(*KIP *joins* 3-YARD *on his knees; they both begin madly searching.)*

GOOEY: *(After a beat; calmly)* I don't seem. To have been answered here.

KIP: *(Pausing)* Maurice got. Lonely. I. Wadn't here. I couldn't come here you know what I? So. She went down to Tomkins and picked up this you get me? This. Blackass. Jujube. And did him. Up here.

GOOEY: Here. Next to our dirt? With the Honduras. On it. Stamped. In neon?

KIP: The dirt was hid, Gooey. Under the sink. Maurice ditn't know. The kid ditn't know. Maurice said she was with him every minute and I believe her.

GOOEY: You do.

KIP: Only.

GOOEY: Only?

(Pause, as KIP *looks away)*

GOOEY: Only you know Maurice was a big one for games. Hey? She had a college degree in sticking her head. Up her ass?

KIP: *(Nodding reluctantly)* Yeah.

3-YARD: *(Pausing in search)* I myself grilled Maurice on this nigger business, Gooey.

GOOEY: *(Examining cigarette)* Get to work, 3-Yard.

(3-YARD does so.)

KIP: But the kid, Gooey. Wears a New York Mets baseball cap and is *not* a professional and plays ball on the nigger side. Of Tomkins Square.

GOOEY: *(Flicking ashes)* It has struck me. In my travels around the metropolitan area. That every negro. Has one of these New York Mets baseball hats. Even their *babies*. Wear these hats.

KIP: But this kid! Has gotta be. A certain. Thing.

3-YARD: *(Pausing again; to KIP)* You know her type?

KIP: *(To 3-YARD)* Sure. A smooth kinna monkey he would have to be. A nipply kinna beast with.

3-YARD: You know your bitch's type?

(GOOEY stares glumly at audience.)

KIP: Like my own teeth. And he would be nipply and very nervous about it and he's no fag.

3-YARD: Not one of these. Basketball butts with the perfume and earrings?

KIP: No way. We are talkin here a kid who peddles loose joints. So he can take some Jamaican whore. To see *Rambo*.

3-YARD: A amateur. Strictly small change.

KIP: But searchlights.

3-YARD: Yeah. Lookin every minute he's lookin.

KIP: He wants? but he don't know how *much*.

3-YARD: He's twenny-five cents but he's hungry.

KIP: Hungry but he don't know for what.

3-YARD: I know the type.

KIP: Could pick him out of a crowd. At a hunnert and ten and Lenox.

3-YARD: You know your bitch's type?

KIP: I have thought about it and I am confident.

3-YARD: I am glad to hear this, Kip.

KIP: Thank you. I am in control.

GOOEY: *(Losing her grip)* Fuck yourselves!

(Silence, as GOOEY *glares at the* 3-YARD *and* KIP. *They abruptly, simultaneously, burrow again into debris.)*

GOOEY: *(With an effort composing herself; rocking)* So. *(Lights one cigarette after another, drops butt on floor; a studied calmness)* The negro? Was just a negro. *(Plucks gum from mouth, jabs it under chair. Crosses her legs, shakes foot. As she rocks, a marked undertone of fear)* You know I got up this morning. And I thought. Don't get started. It's that kinna atmosphere. Here in New York. Today. *(Beat)* It wasn't just the Hertz people. They are paid to be nasty. You go to a competitor it's the American dream. Now it's true that if I had been this shiksa? The poops at Hertz would not have questioned the card. *(Beat)* See. There is this statue. Out in the harbor. Who guarantees. That every piece of shit who comes here? Will be treated with respect. Now Jews. Were never shit. We were the pioneers. The first ones over here. We came in at Angel Island right after they *built* that fuckin statue. We got in our secondhand cars we drove to New Jersey. Long Island. Florida. So I am not whining about the dicks at Hertz. I am just pointing out the historical fact here. *(Checks watch)* You guys got about ten minutes to produce that box.

KIP: *(Pausing)* And then what?

GOOEY: *(Stops rocking)* It's a very uncertain world here, have you noticed? And somebody. *(Exploding) Gotta take charge!*

3-YARD: We're lookin!

KIP: *(Resuming)* We'll find it!

GOOEY: *(Chain-smoking; foot twitching; rocking; new gum)* No, it was on the subway that I knew for sure. Going uptown to Hertz? About the atmosphere. Here today in New York. I was sitting on the I R T uptown local staring at a picture on the door in front of me. There was this "Grotty Eddie 183" written in black ink over the door and on the door was this painting of Mickey Mouse. *(Beat)* With a syringe in his. His hand his mitten you know? It was not a master-piece but it was eyecatchy. Every time there was a stop the doors opened and it disappeared. So you got into the habit. Of watching Mickey Mouse. Appear and disappear. I mean, you know those schwartzers who run the subways? They stop the train at a stop and then sit there for three hours? And they open the doors? And then close the doors. Then they open the doors? Then close the doors. Then open then close *(No pause; a sudden burst of ferocity)* WHO ARE THEY WAITIN FOR, MAHALIA JACKSON???? *(Beat; abruptly calm, rocking and musing)* So anyway. There's this picture of Mickey Mouse with a hypo syringe and I am watching it come and go. The syringe seems to be filled with what looked like to me? Like Haagen-Daaz pistachio ice cream. It made absolutely. No. Sense. *(Beat)* It was an omen of ill-repute *(No pause)* now I do not think. That Maurice. Would bait his hook with a shot of Honduras. For some amateur. *(Shakes head)* Too risky. Not her style. But Maurice *did* know. Where every scrap of shit. Was. In this apartment. She would find the dirt. She would. And she would hide it and eventually. The police will find it. Which is a big pity because they will cut it with chicklets and give it to their wives and brats for Labor Day *(No pause; checking watch)* you got maybe five minutes. *(Beat)* So the question would be. If we had the time to consider it. Is did Maurice. Hide each packet separately or empty all the packets. Say, Into her salt shaker. Or into her douche bag? Or some shit. This is the question if we had the time.

(KIP and 3-YARD look at each other. KIP rushes to cabinets, begins pulling out remaining contents, checks salt and sugar, 3-YARD watches him, then springs into the bedroom.)

GOOEY: *(Not taking notice)* I mean. With a licensed asshole like Maurice. The question would never be. Where is the shoebox?

KIP: *(Tasting sugar, flour, etc)* It ain't here.

GOOEY: Or even maybe her refrigerator.

(KIP plunges into gaping fridge.)

KIP: *(Finding fridge empty)* Eggs. Eggs. All she had was eggs!

(3-YARD emerges from bedroom, trailing a plastic bag by a rubber hose.)

3-YARD: Her hygiene, Gooey. Is very limited and. It's not here.

GOOEY: *(Looking disgustedly at douche bag)* Get! Rid of it.

(3-YARD hastily discards douche bag.)

KIP: This is too. *Obvious!*

GOOEY: *(Rolling up magazine; looking ominously at garbage bag)* I'm gonna kill her.

KIP: Maurice was very underneath! It was a thing of her.

3-YARD: She was a nutzo: History and eggs and shush and lissen and stop the music—

(GOOEY springs to her feet and attacks the garbage bag with rolled-up magazine.)

GOOEY: *The fucking bitch!*

KIP: *(Pulled up short; startled; to 3-YARD)* What. Did you say?

GOOEY: *(Whacking bag) You Protestant dairy queen!*

3-YARD: *(Plunging into debris)* We gotta keep lookin!

KIP: *Shhhh!*

(They all freeze: GOOEY poised to strike bag, 3-YARD to his armpits in magazines. They stare at KIP.)

KIP: *Lissen!* *(Beat)* When the music—

GOOEY: *(Gear-change; flat; to KIP)* Hello?

KIP: *(To himself)* Stops. *(He looks pointedly across stage in direction of discarded radio.)*

GOOEY: Hello? May I speak to asshole? I got a message for him. *Your time! Is running out!*

(KIP stumbles downstage, looks down at radio, lying where 3-YARD had flung it.)

3-YARD: *(To GOOEY, shaking a magazine)* Hey! We should check alla magazines! She coulda pasted our dirt. *Inside!*

GOOEY: *(Mock-excitement)* 3-Yard! This. Is brilliant! *(She picks up a magazine, mock-shakes it in 3-YARD's face, then sits and tears through it, rapidly rocking.)*

(KIP has sunk to his knees, his back to the others. He surreptitiously picks up radio, holds it to his ear, shaking it, wide-eyed: the dope is inside! Meanwhile:)

GOOEY: *Microwave the Protestants!* I ask you *who*, who fucks up the world? Is it Jews? Did I have problems with *Jews* today? No. At the Rent-a-Car? I get this pink smile inna pink shirt questioning my *credit rating!* He had just knoshed on a peanut butter sandwich I could smell it! On his *breath*! I'm tellin you, they are *askin* for it!

3-YARD: *(Desperately shaking magazines)* Check the magazines, lootenant!

KIP: Right! *(He gleefully scatters papers over radio; begins mock-search.)*

GOOEY: *(Ripping pages from magazine, and flinging them over shoulder)* Protestants? Like Maurice? They are everywhere. And they got theories! They got suspicions! They got facts! *(To* 3-YARD*)* Out in Forest Hills???

3-YARD: Yeah?

GOOEY: *THEY GOT TENNIS!* And then they say that *you*! are the neurotical. But I say that *any* race! Who would put peanut butter on a Wonderbun and call it *lunch*? Deserves to get tacked to a cross! Any race that would poop out this mess here—?

KIP: *(Pausing) It's history!*

(Beat; as GOOEY *stares at* KIP*)*

KIP: For Maurice? This was a arkile and a history so shut up!

*(*KIP *glares at* GOOEY, *as she gapes at him. Suddenly* 3-YARD *explodes.)*

3-YARD: *(Flinging papers everywhere)* I hate! All this. SHIT!

*(*KIP *springs upon* 3-YARD, *pushing him away.)*

KIP: *Shut up! (Stands there, hands fisting, breathing hard)*
Maurice knew a lotta stuff and she could tell you!
(Gropes) She could. Tell you.

(Beat; as 3-YARD *and* GOOEY *stare at* KIP*)*

KIP: There was times. When I. Would just. Let her
talk. *(To them)* You guys never knew but! *(He crosses to
sink, grips it, looks into it.)* There was times. When she
would just talk and I would lissen. All kinna about
corporations? And scams they would pull and. Aztecs
and. These very old Greek cocksuckers and.

GOOEY: *(To* 3-YARD*; tapping her watch)* I would rather
have African AIDS. Than listen. To this *shmendrick!*

KIP: *(Angrily spinning round; to* GOOEY*)* And Jews?
She knew more than *you!* With the second-hand cars?
In New Jersey! Than you will ever know about your
own yiddy buncha kikes and lox in your whole fuckin
family!

(A long ugly pause. Finally:)

GOOEY: *(To* 3-YARD*; pointing at* KIP*)* He gonna call me a
beautician again? *Because if he does—!*

3-YARD: We got no time for this!

*(*3-YARD *leaps on a pile of magazines as* KIP *grabs a tray out
of fridge and flings it across the room, after which he laughs
triumphantly. Meantime:)*

GOOEY: I am not! A beautician. What I am, is a hair
stylist!

*(*3-YARD *holds up a magazine.)*

3-YARD: If I see! One more photo! Of some *faggot!* Or
some *president!* Or some cow of a Liz Monroe! In *my*
face! I will personally—! *(He flings away magazine, whips
out shiv, releases blade, heads for bedroom.)*

GOOEY: *(To* 3-YARD*) Where!* Are you going?

(3-YARD *makes a complete turn and marches back to*
GOOEY. *To her:)*

3-YARD: Into the bitch's bedroom. To *murder!* Her
shoes! And her pillows! *(Abruptly he turns from her,*
stomps into bedroom. Through following interchange we
hear, offstage, sounds of slashing and ripping and much
angry grunting.)

(KIP *approaches* GOOEY; *she affects to examine her nails as*
she rocks.)

GOOEY: Okay. Kip you're on what on Rivington today?
So you get your gear we get our gear and we head for
D C. We pick you up say Rivington and the fuckin
Bowery? Hang out on the corner. Give us like. An
hour.

KIP: Rivington and the fuckin Bowery. Is that like.
Where I take the fall?

GOOEY: Don't worry *about* it.

KIP: Answer the question.

GOOEY: *I'll take care of you!* Just like I take care of him.

KIP: You don't run things no more. Get outa that chair.

GOOEY: *(Sniffing the air)* What *is* that?

KIP: I wanna sit down.

GOOEY: *(Same)* Do I smell. A dead. *Hooker?*

(KIP *springs behind rocker, violently pushes it forward.)*

(GOOEY *is flung sprawling onto floor.)*

(KIP *sits in rocker.)*

GOOEY: *(After a beat; looking at audience)* I assume. You
would not have done that. If you hadn't figured out.
(Leaps to her feet; to KIP) *Where it is?*

(KIP *nods.)*

GOOEY: So fuckin let's get on it! We got business! On Long Island!

KIP: Uh-uh. Like you said. A whole new order comin here.

(Beat)

GOOEY: Spit it out, lootenant.

KIP: You mean: *dominator*. *(Beat; casual)* See, Gooey. There's a whole new plan now. See. Now we go to the *other* parties.

GOOEY: The other—?

KIP: The ones you stole the dope off of.

(Beat)

GOOEY: You think I went to all this trouble? To steal from *syndicate*? To risk my knees and shit? Just to give it. *Back?*

KIP: *Def'*unly. And what we gonna do, we gonna put it all on 3-Yard. I tell the injured parties where it's hid here. I say, *we* ditn't steal it. I say 3-Yard stole it. *He* brung the shit to Maurice. Only *we* found out. So *we* took off Maurice. And we will finger 3-Yard for their files.

GOOEY: And then what? *Go ballroom dancing at Roseland?*

KIP: *EAT!* Your lips!

(Beat)

GOOEY: *(Restrained anger)* Okay. Then what?

KIP: Syndicate, Gooey, got some top business people in there, and loyalty is very important in business. And ambition like I'm showin here? Does not grow on walls. They will see this and be very grateful. They will put us onna payroll, Gooey. Then we got a *future*, not

like this one-shot you had planned. And all it takes is I
make a phone call uptown.

GOOEY: Very. Impressive.

(GOOEY *crosses to sink, leans against it. As she does so:*)

KIP: Thank you. Now you may be wondering, Gooey.
Why I have included you here. In my future.

GOOEY: You're sure the dope is here? You saw this
with your own face?

KIP: See. Every dominator gotta have a bitch. Any bitch
would do. Only—

GOOEY: When did you figure out where she hid it? Just
now?

KIP: Only you, Gooey. I will get special cookies. To
see *you*! Legs up. For me. *(Beat)* 3-Yard. Is dead bones.
Drop him at your apartment. By this time I have called
syndicate. You tell 3-Yard you got arrangements to
make and get your ass outa there.

GOOEY: *(Approaching him)* And they will go there and
do laundry with 3-Yard's intestines. And they will
come here and find the dope. And they will give you
and me? A storefront. In Brooklyn. And we will live
happily! *Ever*—!

KIP: *I AM IN CONTROL HERE!* *(Beat)* And this is no.
Bo-de-o. Do.

(Beat; KIP *starts rocking again, as* GOOEY *stares.)*

(Suddenly 3-YARD *emerges from bedroom, covered in
mattress stuffing and down. He halts in the middle of the
room, drops to his knees. Repeatedly he stabs shiv into
magazines and newspapers.)*

3-YARD: *(Rhythmic; to the stabbing action)* We pooped it!
We pooped. Thirt. Teen. Grams. Of horse! We pooped
it. We. Pooped. The deal! *(Stops abruptly, gasping; leaves
shiv in paper and stares at it)*

GOOEY: *(To* KIP; *ignoring* 3-YARD*)* Fuckin you are sure of this?

KIP: *Def* unly.

3-YARD: *I said we pooped it!*

(Beat; as GOOEY *and* KIP *stare at* 3-YARD*)*

3-YARD: Right here. We dropped. On this floor. Thirteen grams of the sweetest. Dirt. I ever. Had a piece of.

*(*GOOEY *turns away in disgust, looks into sink;* KIP *rocks.)*

3-YARD: You don't. Too many times in your life. Look that kinna dope straight inna teeth. You don't. You just. Don't. *(Beat)* I have seen many deals in my time. And rumors of deals. I have heard. Over pool? Some talk. That would curl the hair. On your thighs. But I never. Ever! Heard of a deal so cute. As this. Was. Here. Never! Of a thing like intercepting a shipment? And yankin it off with a commodity this fuckin sweet? Never. Ever. In all my years. On the streets, And pool tables. Of this city. Of Manhattan.

KIP: *(Casually; rocking)* Get up, 3-Yard.

3-YARD: But you unnerstand what I'm talkin here?

KIP: Yeah, I unnerstand.

3-YARD: And you know. That what you said? About how. I was like comin on? To guys! Was a lie. I am hard duty and dick straight right! Down! To my shins.

KIP: Sure. Only. Like Gooey says. We gotta get outa town.

3-YARD: And when a toptool. *Not* a faggot! Loses. A thing like this. He is never. The same. Again.

KIP: We gotta get goin, 3-Yard.

3-YARD: *(Pleading)* Kip, you gotta believe it. Whatever happens? It ain't! *My fault!*

GOOEY: *(Over shoulder; a snapping bark)* 3-Yard!

3-YARD: I'll get up! *(He springs to his feet.)*

(GOOEY takes out keys, flings them over shoulder at 3-YARD.)

GOOEY: Get the car.

KIP: Right. You guys get your gear I'll get mine. Pick me up say. Rivington and the fuckin Bowery. And then on to D C. Right, 3-Yard?

3-YARD: *(Guiltily; picking up keys)* Right. *(Beat)* You're still my lootenant, Kip. I am overlooking. This fucked-up day here. You been the best lootenant. I ever had. *(No response)* So Gooey. You comin? *(No response. Shuffling)* So. This. Is how it ends.

GOOEY: *(Spinning round)* Get! The CAR!

3-YARD: *FUCK* you!

(Beat, as 3-YARD and GOOEY glare. Then she turns away, looks into sink.)

(3-YARD flexes shoulders, jangles keys. Avoiding KIP's gaze, he turns towards door. Pauses by garbage bag:)

3-YARD: I said this. Is how it ends. It comes right here to this. *(Gropes; indicating room)* This arkile history place of a rubber-twatted outrage queen with her duck eggs and fat sucky phobics on Avenue C *(No pause)* it's here! *(Holds up palm of hand, traces words)* It's written right here. That this. Is how. It ends. *(He exits, slamming door behind him.)*

(Beat)

KIP: Gooey? Will you come over here, please?

(GOOEY turns from sink and reluctantly crosses to KIP.)

(He gestures for her to bend down.)

(She bends towards him; he grabs her by the hair, violently, and kisses her brutally on lips. As brutally pushes her away)

KIP: A whole new day. In a whole new thing.

(GOOEY *nervously crouches by rocker, playfully fingering* KIP's *shirt and belt.*)

GOOEY: You know, Kip. If you tell me where it's hid. I can call the injured parties. And take care of all this *for* you.

KIP: Gooey?

GOOEY: Kip?

KIP: On your way back. From droppin off 3-Yard? Before you meet me at, say, Boy Bar? Pick me up a slice. And get one for yourself.

(*Beat;* GOOEY *stiffens. Then she jerks to her feet, crossing towards door. She pauses to stare down, murderously, at garbage bag. Then, to* KIP, *dizzily:*)

GOOEY: See you later? Lovebucket?

KIP: No anchovies.

GOOEY: Pepperoni? Mushroom? (*A bellow:*) Do you like my hair???

(KIP *snaps his fingers.* GOOEY *pops her gum, once, twice, then exits dizzily, slamming door behind her.*)

(*He continues rocking for a beat. Then all at once he springs to his feet, crosses to door and locks it. Turns around, triumphantly, to bag:*)

KIP: You said to get bigger? I *got* bigger. (*He swaggers downstage to radio, uncovering it with his sneaker. Pointing down at it, to bag:*) This was good. To stuff it inna radio. And those clues. The music? The shush and lissen shit? Brilliant. (*Picks up radio, hefting it from hand to hand*) I knew it was in here, soon as I picked it up. (*Shakes radio, next to his ear*) I mean, I kinna knew it was here all along. Cause I am def'unly not. And you knew this, Maurice. I am not some dumboid trippin over his own dick and makin the same stupids over and over. *My*

brain cells. Get busier! When the scene gets fuckier.
And you knew. That I am worth a shitload of this
3-Yard and Gooey. You hadda teach me, Maurice, but
fuckin I got A-plus in history here. *(Crosses to garbage
bag, holding radio; kneels by bag. Tenderly:)* And don't
worry, Maurice. See. This way? The injured parties will
come here. They'll find their merchandise and *(Looking
around)* fix all *this* up? With the cops. You know I
wouldn't'na let you just. Rot here. *(Beat)* You died. So
that I. Could be dominator. *(He rises and with a flourish
unhasps the portable radio. Looks inside. Shock registers on
his face. Slowly he turns radio upside down, and a shower
of newspaper clippings falls to the floor. He shakes it again,
violently. Again looks inside. Stunned; to bag:)* You put
paper in here? You was this yammerhead about. How.
I should lissen to the music when the music stops and
you? Put. *Ann Landers in here? (He snaps shut the radio.)*
Maurice! Long Island gonna radar New York and one!
By one! They gonna pick us *all* off!

(Enraged, KIP *flings radio against the wall; suddenly, it
blares out* Ride of the Valkyries*)*

KIP: Jesus! *(In a panic, he rushes for radio, picks it up,
fiddles madly with the dial, shakes it, bangs in on floor, but
he cannot turn it off. He begins to heap newsprint on top
of it.)* Maurice! Make it stop! *(Hands over ears, he rushes
for door, stumbles, then sprawls among the paper drifts
and debris. Stands, slips, falls again. Finally he reaches
door and yanks at it in vain, forgetting he has locked it. The
music blares.)* Make it stop! *(Finally he remembers and
unlocks door. It catches in the paper. Desperately he yanks it
open, looks once, wildly, at the garbage bag, and then exits,
slamming door behind him.)*

*(The Wagnerian strains continue to fill the stage as lights
slowly dim. Curtain)*

END OF PLAY

www.ingramcontent.com/pod-product-compliance
Lightning Source LLC
Chambersburg PA
CBHW052201090426
42741CB00010B/2358